Track Diagrams - England South and London Underground

These diagrams cover the lines of Network Rail, Southern Region and the London Underground and include a number of private railways and industrial layouts. It is, in general, up-to-date to September 2002. They reflect "operational" c_____

Mileages often vary slightly between different official records, but, in general, those giv_____ been used. Station mileages are usually taken from the mid-point of the platforms, or, in the case of a_____

These diagrams have been compiled substantially from information supplied from v_____ d LUL sources, supplemented by other data and amended from observations. In some cases distinc_____ es are not shown and no inferences concerning ownership should therefore be drawn.

The assistance of numerous Network Rail, London Underground, Docklands and EW&_____. Other acknowledgements are due to the Branch Line Society, the Railway Correspondence &_____ / other correspondents, other railway societies, and also representatives of the other private and pre_____

Please advise the Publisher of further corrections which need to be made.

Cartographer: John Yonge

Consultant editor: Gerald Jacobs

KEY

————	Running line	A broken line indicates 'in situ' but out of use, proposed or under construction (except CTRL)
————	Siding	
——•——	Line obstructed	
——∅——	Change of Line designation	
——o——	Line Out of Use	
	Network Rail Region/Zone boundary	
ER SO		
London Bridge	Ashford	Signal box/centre area limits	
(L) (AD) ASC IECC		
→)– – –(←	Tunnel	
	Viaduct	
	Selected Motorway & Trunk Road bridges over rail	
—+—	Level Crossing (signalled)	} Attributed Number and supervising point may be shown
—ı—	Crossing (telephone or unsignalled)	
←——→	Track signalled in both directions (a double arrow indicates normal direction of travel) (On single lines 'DN' indicates Down direction)	
—⊐	Limit of Electrification	
—⊐	Sand Drag	
—X—	Private siding boundary, often marked by a gate	
—⊖—	Turntable	
∿∿∿∿∿	Wall/Bank	

Electrification Systems, except where otherwise noted

Southern Region	3rd Rail
Eastern Region	OHLE
Midlands Zone	OHLE except ELR 'CWJ'
Great Western Zone	OHLE
CTRL and Trans Manche link etc.	OHLE
LU	4th rail including through running over Network Rail lines

93	Whole mileposts, shown on the appropriate side of the line (for Network Rail)	
32	Whole kilometre posts (for London Underground, CTRL, etc) usually on the appropriate side of the line	
81.3	End of mileage run	
3 8	Platform with number and accommodation in coaches (approx 20m lengths)	
⌐ _ _ ⌐	Provisional proposed platform	
▭	Royal Mail Platform	
	Platform out of use (or proposed on CTRL)	
▨	Loading Bank	
⊠ (L)	Signal box or Signalling Centre, with code (name underlined)	
◩	Gate box	
⊡	Ground frame or Shunting Frame	
⊕	Radio Electronic Token Block - Token Exchange Point	
○	Water Tower	
∧	Summit	
•	Location spot	
86.34	Distance in miles and chains (80 chains to 1 mile; 22 yards - about 20 metres - equal 1 chain)	
86·34	Distance in Kilometres (Eurotunnel, CTRL, London Underground)	
BML	ELR (Engineers Line Reference) Prefix and suffix numbers indicate sub-divisions and their boundaries	
SW 105	Line of Route Code	

Guide references may be given to pre-nationalisation, pre-grouping and sometimes pioneer railways e.g. S: LSW (London and Southampton). References to adjoining volumes and page numbers refer to previously published books and will not necessarily be the same in future editions.

LONDON UNDERGROUND SIGNALLING

LU signalling is controlled at some places by local Signal Cabins, or for a long part or the whole of some lines by Signal Control Centres.

Because of different cables, LU has Interlocking Machines operated by air motors (or comparable equipment) in unmanned rooms near some points, except where a local cabin has an interlocking lever frame. IMR's (and equivalent rooms) are included in these maps, but purely Relay Rooms (and their equivalents) are not. IMR's bear the name of the adjacent station unless otherwise noted: (e) indicates location at the end of the platform, (m) in the middle of the platform.

▢ (MAA)	Local Cabin or Control Centre with code(s) controlled	(NP)	Interlocking inside former cabin
(MU)	Unmanned Interlocking Machine (or comparable equipment) Room with code.	⊡	Ground Frame
(NP)	Interlocking within manned cabin with code(s) controlled	ı BR | BS	Code area boundaries (where not separated by a long stretch of plain track(s))
		(TK)/(CAW)	Signal Area/Station Identity

PRICE £8.95   ISBN: 1 898319 52 9

Published by the Quail Map Company, 2 Lincoln Road, Exeter EX4 2DZ (Telephone/Fax: 01392 430277)
and printed by the Brightsea Press Ltd, Exeter
© John Yonge, Gerald Jacobs and The Quail Map Company. September 2002

GENERAL ABBREVIATIONS

AA	Acid Application	MSL(B)(F)	Miniature Stop Lights with (B) Barriers, (F) Footpath,
ABCL	Automatic Barrier Crossing - (Locally monitored)	(G)	(G) Gates
ABP	Associated British Ports	N	North
AHB	Automatic Half Barriers	n	Not electrified
AOCL	Automatic Open Crossing - (Locally monitored)	NB	Northbound
AOCR	Automatic Open Crossing - (Remotely monitored)	NIRU	Not in regular use
ARR	Arrival	NR	Network Rail
ASC	Area Signalling Centre i/c IECC, Power Box	OC	Open Crossing
bdy	boundary	OHC	Overhead crane
BCH	Branch	OHLE	Overhead Line Equipment
BR	British Rail	OOU	Out of use
CCTV	Closed Circuit television	Open	Open crossing - no lights
CET	Controlled Emission Toilet Discharge	OTM	On-track Maintenance
CL	Crossing Loop on Single Line	P	Points padlocked
COM	Change of Mileage	PAD	Prefabricated Assembly Depot
CR	Cripple siding	PL	Passenger Loop
CW	Carriage washer	PS	Private siding
C&W	Carriage & Wagon	PSB	Power signal box
D	Connections Disconnected	PW	Permanent Way
DA	Down Avoiding	Qy	Query concerning distances etc, unresolved
DE	Down Electric	RC	Remotely controlled
DEP	Departure	REC	Reception
DF	Down Fast	RES	Rail Express Systems
DG	Down Goods	RETB	Radio Electronic Token Block
DGL	Down Goods Loop	REV	Reversing or Reversible line
DM	Down Main	R/G	Miniature red/green warning lights
DN	Down	RR	Run-round
DPL	Down Passenger Loop	RT	Railtrack
DR	Down Relief	S	South
DRS	Down Refuge Sidings	SB	Signal box or Southbound
DS	Down Slow	SC	Signalling Centre
DSB	Down Surbutan	Sdg(s)	Siding(s)
E	East	SD	Sand Drag
e	electrified	SF	Shunting Frame
EB	Eastbound	SN	Shunt Neck
EGF	Emergency Ground Frame	SP	Switch Panel
EMU	Electric multiple-unit	SS	Shunt Spur
Engrs	Engineers' sidings	TA	Tamper siding
eol	End of Line	TB	Turnback Siding
ESP	Emergency Signalling Panel	TEP	Token Exchange Point
EW & S	English Welsh & Scottish Railway Ltd	TL	Traffic lights
FA	Flushing Apron	TMD	Traction Maintenance Depot
FP	Fuelling point or Footpath	TMO	Traincrew operated
ft	Feet	TR&SMD	Traction & Rolling Stock Maintenance Depot
GB	Gate Box	U&D	Up & Down
GDS	Goods	UA	Up Avoiding
GF	Ground Frame	UE	Up Electric
GL	Goods loop	UF	Up Fast
GS	Goods Shed	UFN	Until Further Notice
GSP	Ground Switch Panel	UG	Up Goods
H	Headshunt	UGL	Up Goods Loop
HH	Hopper House	UH	Unloading Hopper
HST	High Speed Train	UM	Up Main
IECC	Intergrated Electronic Control Centre	UPL	Up Passenger Loop
Jn	Junction	UR	Up Relief
Jt	Joint	URS	Up Refuge Siding
Km	kilometres	US	Up Slow
L	Wheel Lathe	USB	Up Suburban
LC	Level Crossing (manned, automatic or open)	UT	Up Through
LHS	Loco. Holding Siding	UWB	User-worked Barriers
LP	Loop	UWC(m)	User-worked crossing (m-miniature R/G Warning lights)
LPG	Liquified petroleum gas	UWG	User-worked Gates
LS	Locomotive shed	V or Vdct	Viaduct
LW	Locomotive Washer	W	West
M	Middle	WB	Westbound or Weighbridge
MB/MCB	Manned/Manually, Controlled/Operated, Barriers	WD	War Department
MGW	Manned/Manually, Controlled/Operated, Gates (with Wickets)	X	(After level crossing type abbreviations) - the crossing works automatically for movements in the wrong direction
MGR	'Merry-go-round'		
MN	Main	yds	yards

SUPPLEMENTARY ABBREVIATIONS FOR THIS BOOK

CTRL	Channel Tunnel Rail Link	LU	London Underground Limited
		MD	Midlands Zone
ER	Eastern Region	MSW	former Midland and South Western Jn Railway
ET	Eurotunnel	N&SWJn	former North and South Western Jn Railway
GC	former Great Centra Railway	RFF	Réseau Ferré de France
GE	former Great Eastern Railway	S	former Southern Railway
GN	former Great Northern Railway	SE	former South Eastern Railway
GW	Great Western Zone or former Great Western Railway	SNCF	Société Nationale des Chemins de Fer Français (French National Railways)
LBSC	former London, Brighton and South Coast Railway	SO	Southern Region
LCD	former London, Chatham and Dover Railway		
LGV	Ligne à Grande Vitesse (High Speed line)	TGV	Train à Grande Vitesse (High Speed Train)
LMS	former London Midland and Scottish Railway		
LNE	former London and North Eastern Railway	WL	former West London Joint Railway
LNW	former London and North Western Railway	WLE	former West London Extension Joint Railway
LPTB	former London Passenger Transport Board		
LSW	former London and South Western Railway		

ENGINEERS LINE REFERENCES

ELR	ROUTE DESCRIPTION

ELR	Route Description
	Ascot Jn - Ash Vale Jn
	Ashford 'E' Jn - Canterbury West - Ramsgate
	Acton Canal Wharf - Willesden
	Angerstein Jn - Angerstein Wharf
	Nine Elms Jn - Linford Street Jn
	Alton - Winchester Jn
	Addlestone Jn - Byfleet Jn
	Acton and Northolt line (via Greenford East)
	Appledore - Lydd Town - Dungeness
	Turnham Green (LU Bdy) - Gunnersbury Jn
	Ashford 'D' Jn - Hastings
	Peckham Rye - Battersea Park Jn (Atlantic line/South London line)
	Acton East - Acton Wells Jn.
	Basingstoke (Worting Jn) - Exeter St Davids
	Bricklayers Arms Branch (Closed)
	Bournemouth West Carriage Sidings
	Balham Jn - Beckenham Jn
	Barnham Jn - Bognor Regis
	Brent Curve Jn. - Dudding Hill Jn.
	St. Johns Jn - Crayford Creek Jn via Bexleyheath
	Berks and Hants line (Southcote Jn - Patney & Westbury Jn)
	Bromley Jn - Norwood Jn
	Basingstoke Branch (Reading Westbury line Jn - Basingstoke
	Brighton (West Coast) - Littlehampton
	Brockenhurst - Lymington Pier
	Buckland Jn - Minster East Jn
	Blackfriars Jn - Metropolitan Jn
	Waterloo (Main lines) - Weymouth (Bournemouth Main line)
	Bromley North - Grove Park Jn
	Broad Street (Closed) - Old Kew Jn via Hampstead Heath (North London line)
	Lovers Walk Depot
	Battersea Pier Jn (LCD) - Stewarts Lane - Factory Jn
	Battersea Pier Jn (LBSC) - Stewarts Lane - Longhedge Jn - Pouparts Jn
	Blackheath Jn - Charlton Jn
	Barking: Tilbury line Jn East - Barking East Jn
	South Bermondsey Jn - Sutton - Epsom - Horsham Jn
	Brighton (East Coast) - Lewes Jn
	Barking W. Jn - Barking Tilbury line Jn West
	Brixton Jn - Catford - Shortlands Jn (Catford Loop)
	Cricklewood Curve Jn. - Acton Wells Jn.
	Cannon Street - Borough Market Jn
	Castle Cary and Langport line
	Copyhold Jn - Ardingly
	Clapham Jn (Ludgate Jn) - Latchmere No.2 Jn
	Longhedge Jn (Calvert Rd Jn) - Latchmere No.1 Jn
	Chart Leacon, Ashford, Depot
	Clapham Junction Sidings
	Crayford Spur 'B' Jn - Crayford Spur 'A' Jn
	Chislehurst - St. Mary Cray Jn (Chatham Loops)
	Metropolitan Jn - Cannon Street South Jn
	Camden Jn - Watford Jn.(DC Electric lines)
	Gillingham (Kent) - Chatham Dockyard
	Exeter and Devonport line (via Okehampton) (Devon and Cornwall)
	Eastleigh East Jn - (Chandler's Ford) - Romsey Jn
	Shepherdswell - Tilmanstone Cly (EKLR)
	Exmouth Jn - Exmouth
	Eastleigh West Jn - Fareham East Jn
	Eastleigh Yards etc.
	Faversham - Dover (former Hawkesbury St. Jn)
	Folkestone East Jn - Folkestone Harbour
	Farlington Jn - Cosham Jn
	Ford Jn - Littlehampton Jn
	Factory Jn - Longhedge Jn - Lavender Hill Jn - Clapham (Ludgate Jn)
	Fenchurch Street - Shoeburyness
	Fareham West Jn - Bedenham Sidings

ELR	Route Description
FTL	Farringdon Jn - (Ludgate) Blackfriars
FUR	Worgret Jn - Furzebrook Sidings
GEC	Greenford East Curve
GTW	Guildford North Jn - Wokingham Jn
HAG	Hamworthy Jn. - Hamworthy Goods
HAM	Surbiton (Down Hampton Court Line Jn) - Hampton Court
HDR	Hither Green Jn - Dartford - Rochester Bridge Jn
HGG	Hurst Green Jn - East Grinstead
HGP	Hither Green/Grove Park Sidings
HHH	(Holborn Viaduct) Blackfriars - Herne Hill South Jn
HHT	Herne Hill South Jn - Tulse Hill South Jn
HJW	Hounslow Jn - Whitton Jn
HOU	Barnes Jn - Hounslow - Feltham Jn (Hounslow Loop)
HSE	Hawkesbury Street Jn - Archcliffe Jn
HTG	Hoo Jn - Grain
IOW	Ryde Pier Head - Shanklin (Isle of Wight)
JAT	Waterloo International
LBC	London Bridge (Platforms 14-16) - Bricklayers Arms Jn (South London Spur line)
LBW	London Bridge (Platforms 8-13) - Windmill Bridge Jn
LCH	Lewisham East Jn (Ladywell line) - Hayes
LEC	London, Euston - Crewe
LEE	Lee Jn - Lee Spur Jn
LEJ	Leatherhead Jn - Effingham Jn
LLG	Willesden, West London Jn. - Sudbury Jn. (Low Level Goods)
LLL	Parks Bridge Jn - Ladywell Jn (Ladywell Loop)
LOC	Loughborough Jn - Canterbury Road Jn
LTC	Loughborough Jn - Cambria Jn
LTH	Leigham Jn - Tulse Hill Jn (Leigham Spur)
LUD	Andover - Ludgershall
LVT	Lewisham Vale Jn - Tanners Hill Jn
MCJ	Marylebone - Claydon LNE Jn via Harrow-on-the-Hill
MCL	Kentish Town Jn - Moorgate (Midland City line)
MIS	Millbrook - Southampton Western Docks
MLN	Paddington - Bristol - Penzance ('Main Line')
MOD	Dinton East Jn - Chilmark
MPC	Motspur Park - Chessington South
MSW	Minster South Jn - Minster West Jn
NAJ	Neasden South Jn. - Aynho Jn
NBB	New Beckenham Jn - Beckenham Jn
NCS	Courthill Loop Jn North - Courthill Loop Jn South (Courthill Loop)
NFE	Norwood Jn (Wallington Line Jn) - Epsom Downs
NGL	Hampton Court Jn - Guildford, New Line Jn (New Guildford Line)
NHB	Newhaven Harbour Jn - Newhaven Harbour
NJN	Neasden Curve
NKE	New Kew Jn. - Kew East Jn.
NKL	North Kent East Jn - Greenwich - Dartford Jn
NMS	New Malden Jn - Shepperton
NSA	Aldershot South Jn - Aldershot North Jn
NTL	Nunhead Jn - Lewisham Jn
NYD	Norwood Yard and Selhurst Workshop Sidings
OJS	Otford Jn - Sevenoaks Jn
PAA	Pirbright Jn - Alton
PAS	Portsmouth, Blackfriars Jn - Portsmouth & Southsea Low Level
PAT	Purley - Caterham
PBE	Putney Bridge (former LU Bdy) - East Putney Jn
PPH	Preston Park - Hove
PPW	Point Pleasant Jn - Wimbledon (LU platforms)
PSF	Perry Street Fork Jn - Slade Green Jn
PWS	Paddock Wood - Strood

ELR	Route Description
RDG	Waterloo (Windsor lines) - Reading
RED	Stoats Nest Jn - Redhill - Earlswood Jn (Redhill line)
RNJ	Reading Spur Jn - Reading New Jn
RPE	Raynes Park Jn - Epsom Jn
RSJ	Redhill, Guildford Line Jn - Shalford Jn
RTJ	Redbridge Jn - Salisbury, Tunnel Jn
RTT	Redhill, Tonbridge Line Jn - Tonbridge West Jn
RWC	Reading West Curve
SAL	Westbury South Jn - Wilton Jn (Salisbury Branch)
SAR	South Acton Jn - Richmond
SBJ	Swanley Jn - Ashford 'B' Jn via Maidstone East
SCC	West London Jn - Latchmere No.3 Junction (Sheepcote Curve)
SCP	Sydenham Jn - Crystal Palace, Tunnel Jn
SCU	South Croydon Jn - Uckfield
SDP	St Denys Jn - Portcreek Jn
SEJ	Sittingbourne, Eastern Jn - Sheerness
SHF	Strawberry Hill Jn - Fulwell Jn
SLC	Stewarts Lane Sidings
SLJ	Streatham North Jn (Slow lines) - Streatham South Jn (Slow lines)
SLT	Stonebridge Park - LU Depot
SMS	Streatham South Jn - Sutton, Wimbledon Line or West Jn (via Wimbledon)
SNS	Streatham North Jn (Fast line) - Streatham South Jn (Fast line)
SOY	Northam Jn - Southampton Eastern Docks
SSC	Streatham Jn - Streatham Common Jn
STS	Southerham Jn - Seaford
SWE	Staines Jn - Windsor & Eton Riverside
SWY	Stert and Westbury line, Patney and Chirton - Westbury
TAH	Tottenham and Hampstead
TAT	Purley (Chipstead Line) Jn - Tattenham Corner
TBH	Three Bridges Jn - Havant Jn via Horsham
TLL	Tilbury Loop Line
TLP	Bickley Jn - Petts Wood Jn (Tonbridge Loops)
TML	Saltwood Jn/Continental - Eurotunnel boundary (Trans-Manche Link)
TSJ	Twickenham Jn - Shacklegate Jn
TTF	Totton - Fawley
TTH	Tonbridge East Jn - Hastings
UHL	Wembley Yard - Willesden (Up High Level Arrival Line)
USY	Up Sidings Yard, Westbury
VIR	Victoria (Eastern) - Ramsgate via Herne Hill and Chatham
VTB	Victoria (Central) - Brighton via Streatham Common and Quarry Line
VWW	Virginia Water - Weybridge
WAW	Willesden, Low Level Goods Jn. - Acton Wells Jn.
WCL	Willesden - Willesden Carriage Shed North via Carriage Lines
WCS	Selhurst Jn - Gloucester Road Jn
WES	Westbury Avoiding Line
WEY	Thingley Jn - Dorchester Jn (Weymouth Line)
WGS	Willesden Inter City Depot
WJB	Willingden Jn - Bopeep Jn
WKG	Woking Yard
WLL	Clapham Jn, Falcon Jn. - Willesden, West London Jn. (West London Line)
WMB	Willesden High Level Jn. - Mitre Bridge Jn.
WMS	Sittingbourne Western Jn - Middle Jn
WPH	Woking Jn - Portsmouth Harbour (Portsmouth Direct line)
WPK	Wimbledon Park and Depot Sidings
WTH	West Norwood Jn - Tulse Hill Jn (West Norwood Spur)
WTQ	Weymouth Jn - Weymouth Quay
WTS	Willesden Through Sidings: Harlesden to Brent
WYL	Westbury East Loop
WZS	Willesden Traction Maintenance Depot Sdgs
XTD	Charing Cross - Dover (former Archcliffe Jn) via Chelsfield
YJP	Yeovil Pen Mill Jn - Yeovil Jn

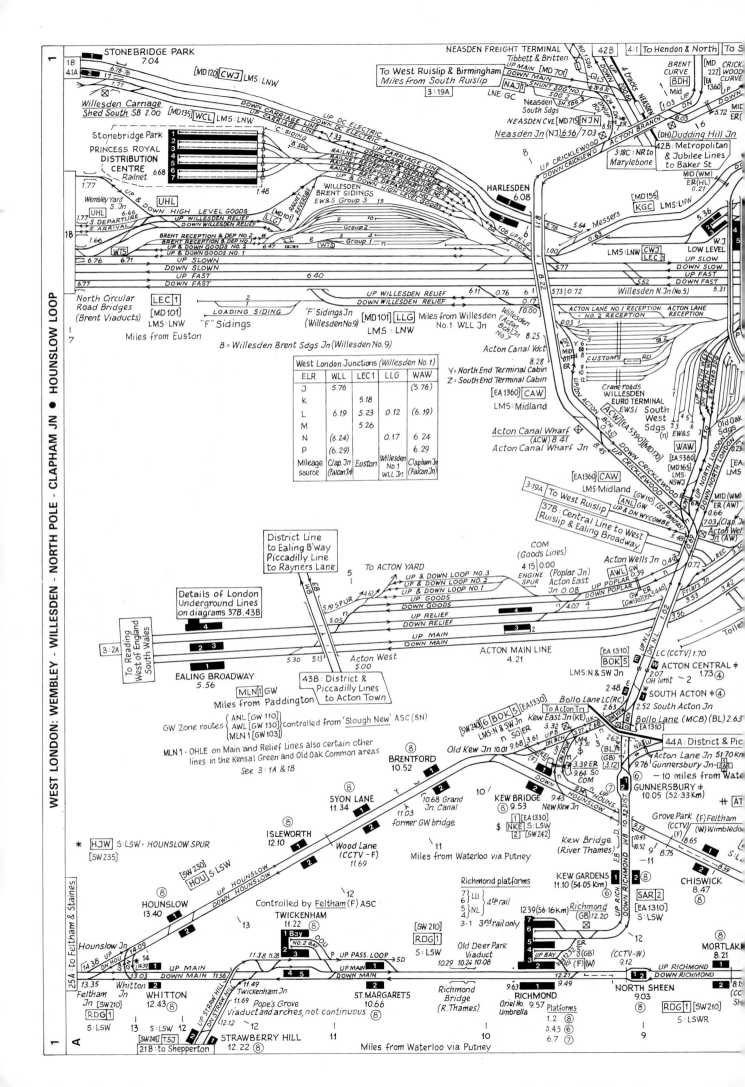

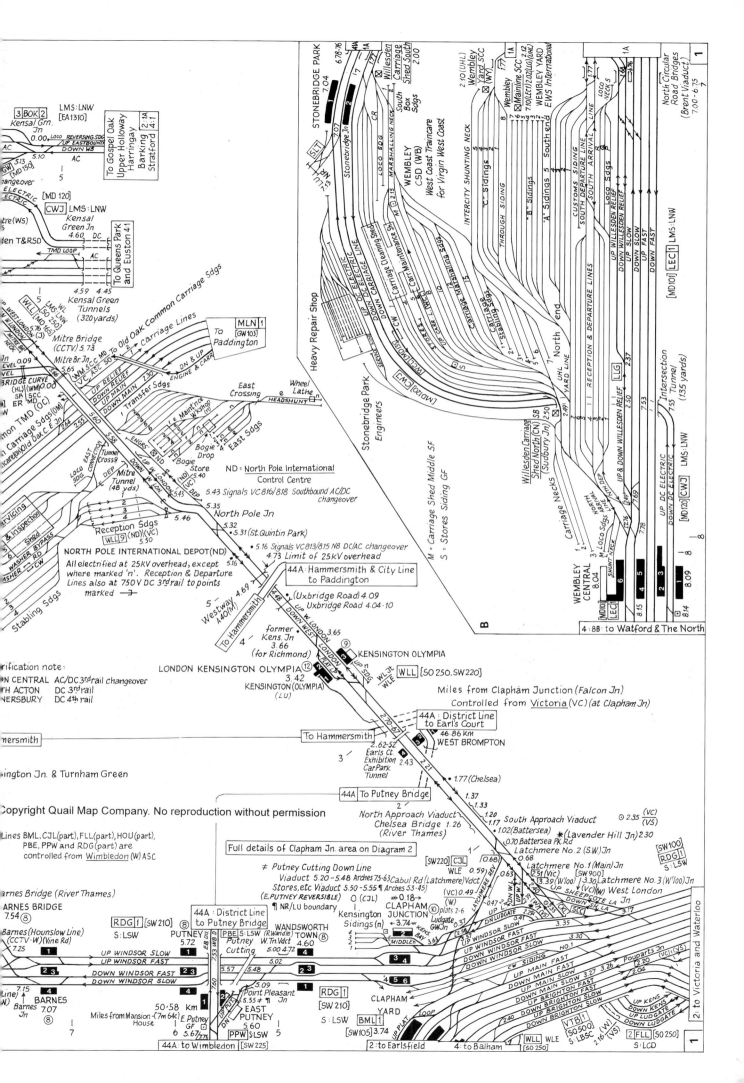

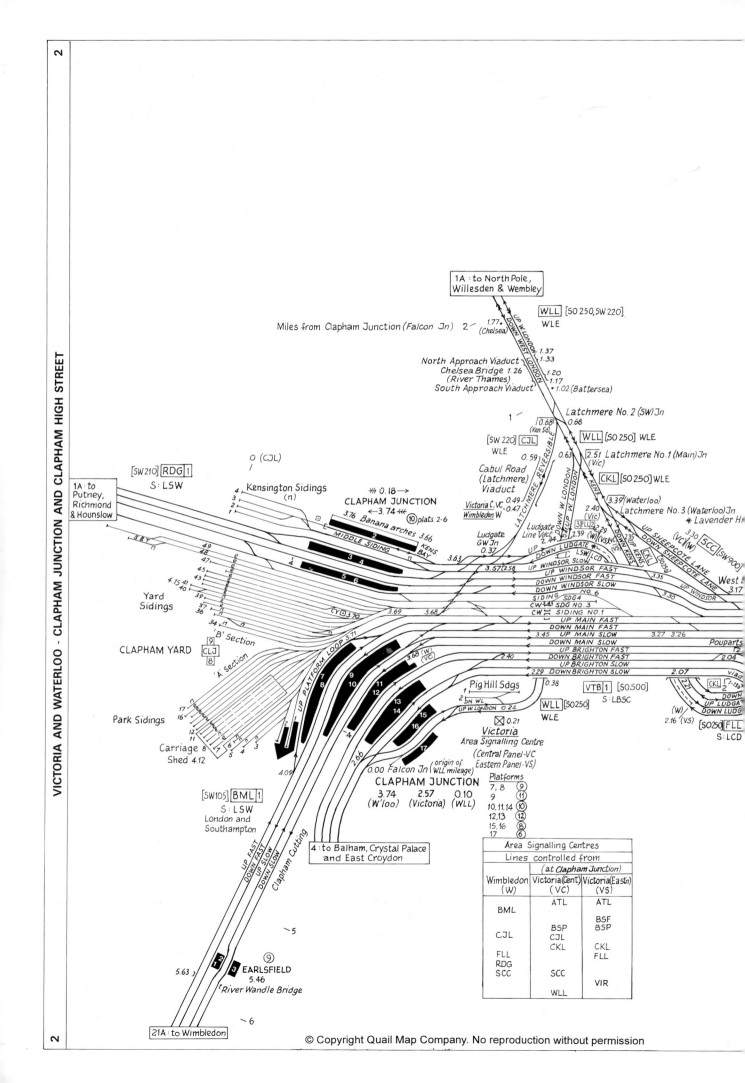

1A : to North Pole,
Willesden & Wembley

WLL [SO 250, SW 220]
WLE

Miles from Clapham Junction (Falcon Jn) 2 — 1.77 •
(Chelsea)

North Approach Viaduct
Chelsea Bridge 1.26
(River Thames)
South Approach Viaduct

1.37
1.33
1.20
1.17
• 1.02 (Battersea)

Latchmere No. 2 (SW) Jn
1 — 0.68
(0.68)
(Ken Sdg)

[SW 220] CJL
WLE
WLL [SO 250] WLE

2.51 Latchmere No. 1 (Main) Jn
(Vic)

Cabul Road
(Latchmere)
Viaduct

0.59
0.63

CKL [SO 250] WLE

[SW 210] RDG 1
S : LSW

O (CJL)

0.49
0.47

Victoria C.VC
Wimbledon W

(3.39) (Waterloo)
2.40 Latchmere No. 3 (Waterloo) Jn
(Vic)

* Lavender H!

Kensington Sidings
(n)

⋙ 0.18 ⟶

CLAPHAM JUNCTION
← 3.74 ⋘

⑩ plats. 2-6

Ludgate
GW Jn
0.37

Ludgate
Line Vdct
2.44

2.29
3 FLL
(W)
2.39 (W)

3.30 (VC) (W)
3.17

SCC [SW 900]

West !

1A : to
Putney, Richmond
& Hounslow

3.76 Banana arches 3.66
MIDDLE SIDING

KENS.
BAY

3.63

3.57 2.58
UP WINDSOR SLOW
UP WINDSOR FAST
DOWN WINDSOR FAST
DOWN WINDSOR SLOW
SIDING SDG4
NO. 6

3.35

UP WINDSOR

S.&T.

4.9
4.8
4.7

3 4

1

5 6

CY ⊡ 3.70

4.5
4.3
4.15 41
40

39
37
36

3.69
3.68

CW ≒ SDG NO. 3
CW ⊟ SIDING NO.1
UP MAIN FAST
DOWN MAIN FAST

3.30

Yard
Sidings

34 □

'B' Section

9
CLJ
8

'A' Section

3.45 UP MAIN SLOW
DOWN MAIN SLOW
UP BRIGHTON FAST
DOWN BRIGHTON FAST
UP BRIGHTON SLOW
2.29 DOWN BRIGHTON SLOW

3.27 3.26

3.30

Pouparts

2.04

viac

CLAPHAM YARD

UP PLATFORM LOOP 3.71

3.68 (W)
(VC)

2.40

7 8
9
10
11
12
13
14 15
16

2.07

CKL
7 130

2.27

Park Sidings

3.68 (W)
(VC)

DN WL
UP W.LONDON 0.24

Pig Hill Sdgs

0.38

VTB 1 [SO 500]
S : LBSC

2
DOWN
UP LUDGATE
DOWN LUDG.

17
16
15
12
11
9

7 6 5 4 3 2 1

2

⊠ 0.21

WLL [SO 250]
WLE

(W)
2.16 (VS)

[SO 250] FLL
S : LCD

Carriage 8
Shed 4.12

4.09

1

Victoria
Area Signalling Centre
(Central Panel-VC
Eastern Panel-VS)

0.00 Falcon Jn
(origin of
WLL mileage)

2.66

[SW 105] BML 1
S : LSW
London and
Southampton

CLAPHAM JUNCTION
3.74   2.57   0.10
(W'loo) (Victoria) (WLL)

Platforms	
7, 8	⑨
9	⑪
10, 11, 14	⑩
12, 13	⑫
15, 16	⑧
17	⑥

4 : to Balham, Crystal Palace
and East Croydon

Area Signalling Centres		
Lines controlled from		
	(at *Clapham Junction*)	
Wimbledon (W)	Victoria (Cent) (VC)	Victoria (East'n) (VS)
BML	ATL	ATL
		BSF
	BSP	BSP
CJL	CJL	
	CKL	CKL
FLL		FLL
RDG		
SCC	SCC	
		VIR
	WLL	

UP FAST
DOWN FAST
UP SLOW
DOWN SLOW
Clapham Cutting

— 5

⑨

1 2
3

EARLSFIELD
5.46
River Wandle Bridge

5.63)

— 6

21A : to Wimbledon

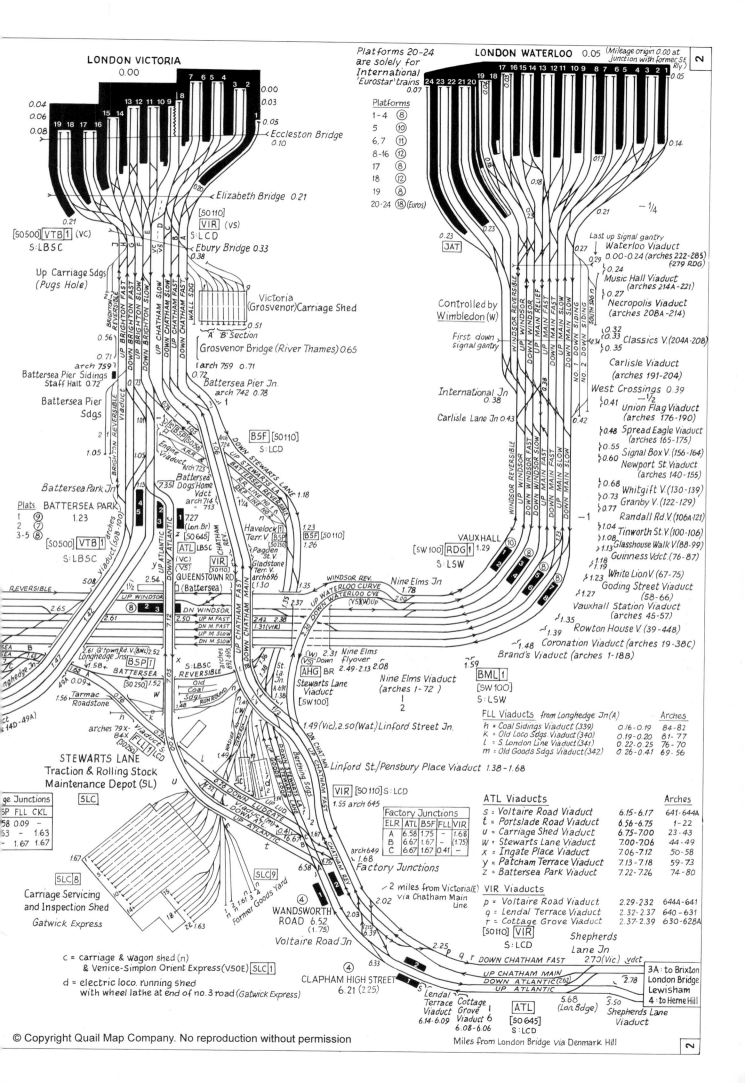

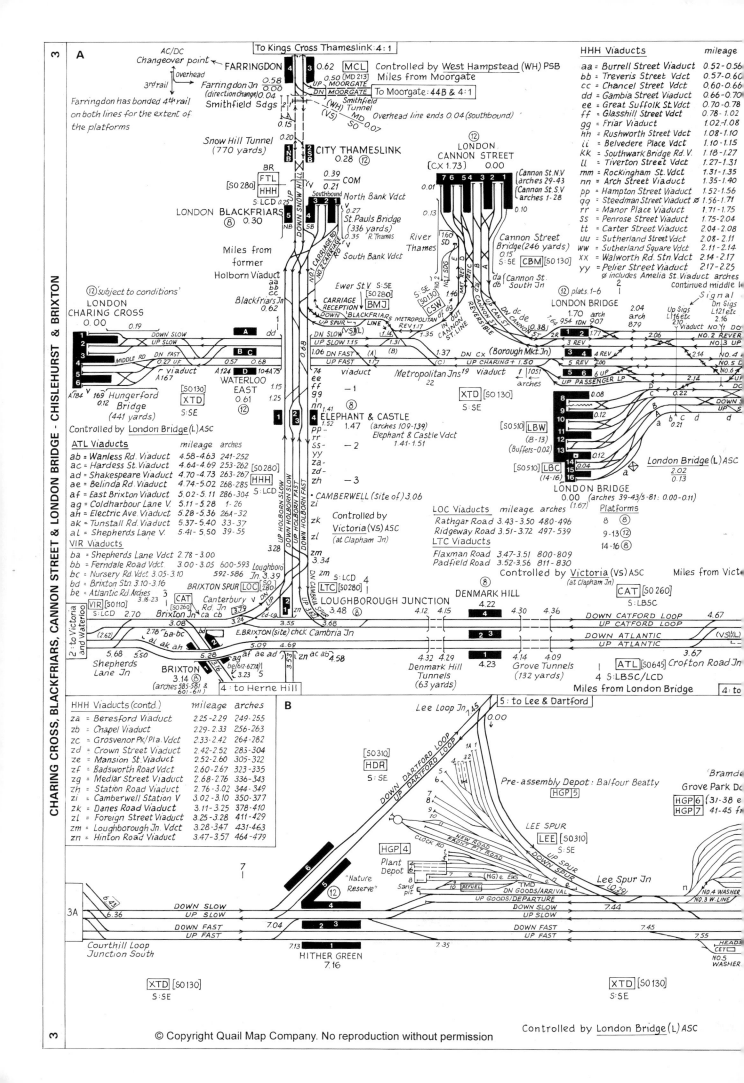

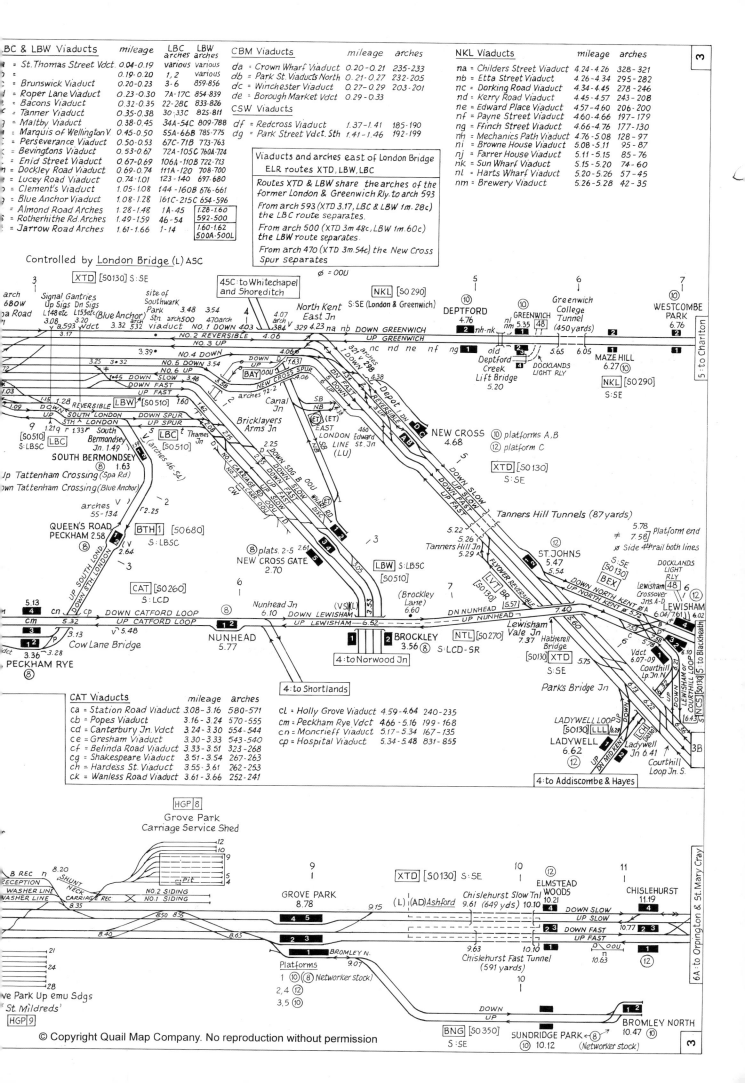

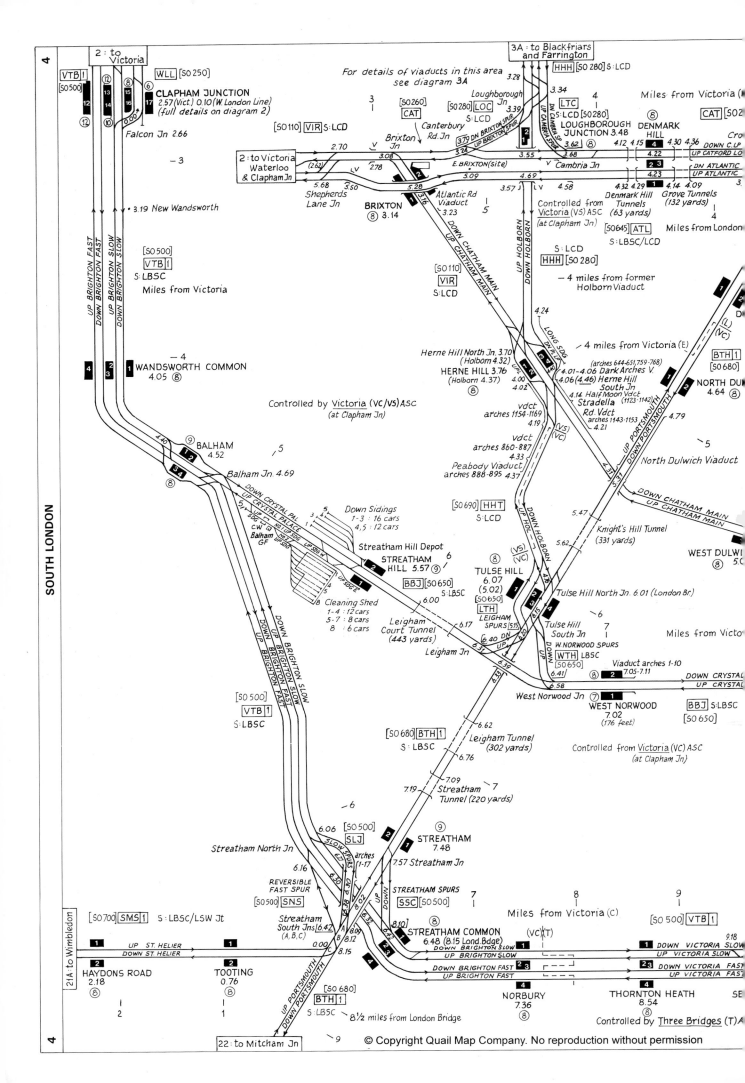

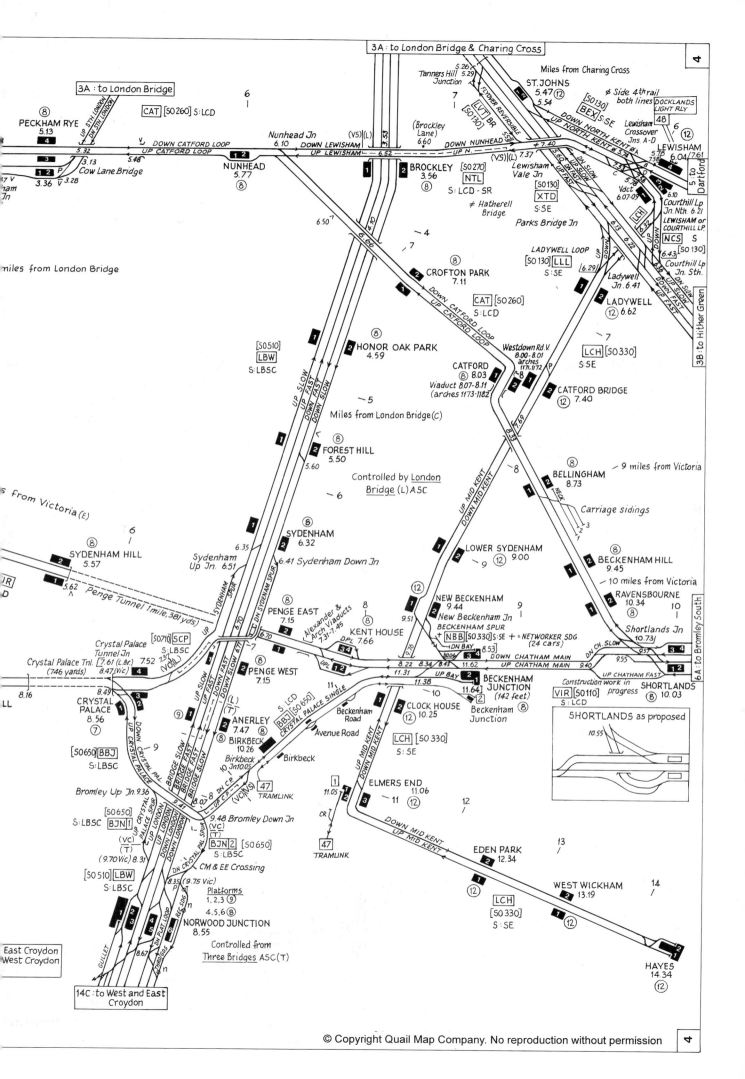

3A: to London Bridge & Charing Cross

Miles from Charing Cross

3A: to London Bridge

Tanners Hill Junction 5.26 5.29

ST. JOHNS 5.47 ⑫ 5.54

Ø Side 4th rail both lines

DOCKLANDS LIGHT RLY 48 ⑫

Lewisham Crossover Jns. A-D

LEWISHAM 6.04/7.61 ④

5: to Dartford

⑧ PECKHAM RYE 5.13 ■④

CAT [SO 260] S: LCD

UP STH LONDON DN STH LONDON

LVT BR [SO 130]

FLYOVER REVERSIBLE

BEX S·SE [SO 130]

UP NORTH KENT DOWN NORTH KENT

+ 7.40

DOWN CATFORD LOOP 5.32

UP CATFORD LOOP 5.48

Nunhead Jn 6.10

DOWN LEWISHAM (VS)(L)

(Brockley Lane) 6.60

DOWN NUNHEAD 5.58

DN FAST UP FAST

7.53 6.62 DN SLOW

5.78 6.28

Courthill Lp Jn. Nth. 6.21

■③ 3.13

Cow Lane Bridge 5.48

■1 2 P

UP LEWISHAM — 6.52

UP N.

① BROCKLEY 3.56 ⑧ [SO 270]

(VS)(L) 7.37

Lewisham Vale Jn 5.62

Vdct 6.07-09 LCH

LEWISHAM or COURTHILL LP.

7 3.36 V 3.28

② BROCKLEY

[SO 270] NTL

S: LCD-SR

≠ Hatherell Bridge

[SO 130] XTD S:SE

UP FAST 6.13 6.22

Courthill Lp Jn. Sth. 6.43

NC5 [SO 130] S

7 V

am Jn

6.50 7

4.10

6.66

4

7

Parks Bridge Jn

6.29

DOWN SLOW

UP SLOW

miles from London Bridge

⑧ CROFTON PARK 7.11

② ① 8.73

LADYWELL LOOP [SO 130] LLL S:SE

① Ladywell Jn. 6.41

② LADYWELL ⑫ 6.62

[SO 510] LBW S: LBSC

① ② HONOR OAK PARK 4.59

① CAT [SO 260] S: LCD

CATFORD ⑧ 8.03

Westdown Rd. V. 8.00-8.01 arches 1171,1172

① ② P

LCH [SO 330] S:SE

7

Viaduct 8.07-8.11 (arches 1173-1182)

CATFORD BRIDGE ⑫ 7.40

UP SLOW DOWN FAST DOWN SLOW

5

Miles from London Bridge (C)

① ⑧ FOREST HILL 5.50

5.60

6

8.33

UP MID KENT DOWN MID KENT

8

⑧ BELLINGHAM 8.73

9 miles from Victoria

Carriage sidings

① ⑧ SYDENHAM 6.32

② SYDENHAM

miles from Victoria (E)

6

⑧ SYDENHAM HILL 5.57

②

① 5.62

Penge Tunnel (mile, 381 yds)

Sydenham Up Jn. 6.51

6.35

6.41 Sydenham Down Jn

DN SYDENHAM SPUR UP SYDENHAM SPUR

① LOWER SYDENHAM ⑫ 9.00

9

②

①

② BECKENHAM HILL 9.45

10 miles from Victoria

② RAVENSBOURNE 10.34 10

Shortlands Jn 10.73

⑫

① NEW BECKENHAM 9.44 ② New Beckenham Jn 9.51

BECKENHAM SPUR

NBB [SO 330] S:SE + = NETWORKER SDG (24 cars)

DN CH. SLOW 9.55 9.57

③④

SYDENHAM SPUR

PENGE EAST 7.15

⑧

Alexander & Arch Viaducts 7.31-7.45

KENT HOUSE 7.66

8 8

DN BAY ① DPL

8.53

Crystal Palace Tunnel Jn 7.52 7.61 (L.br.)

[SO 710] SCP S:LBSC

(VC)(L)

DN SLOW 6.77

①

8.22 8.34 8.43

④

DOWN CHATHAM MAIN 11.62 UP CHATHAM MAIN 9.40

UP CHATHAM FAST

① ②

6A: to Bromley South

Crystal Palace Tnl. (746 yards)

8.47 (Vic) ④

② PENGE WEST 7.15

UP PGL

11.31

UP BAY

⑧ BECKENHAM JUNCTION 11.64

Construction work in progress

SHORTLANDS 10.03

8.16

8.49

③ ②

① CRYSTAL PALACE 8.56 ⑦

[SO 650] BBJ S: LBSC

ANERLEY 7.47 ⑧

① 9 ⑧

BIRKBECK 10.26

11.38

Beckenham Road

② CLOCK HOUSE ⑫ 10.25

10

Beckenham Junction

⑧

VIR [SO 110] S: LCD

SHORTLANDS as proposed

10.55

UP SLOW DOWN FAST BRIDGE FAST BRIDGE SLOW

LL

Birkbeck Jn 10.05

Birkbeck

Avenue Road

LCH [SO 330] S:SE

Bromley Up Jn. 9.36

(L)(T)

S: LCD BBJ [SO 650]

CRYSTAL PALACE SINGLE

UP CRYSTAL PAL.

(VC)(VS) 47 TRAMLINK

11 ① 11.05

ELMERS END 11.06

12

[SO 650] BJN 1 S: LBSC

(VC)(T)

(9.70 Vic) 8.31

9.48 Bromley Down Jn (VC)(T)

BJN 2 [SO 650] S: LBSC

DN CRYSTAL PAL SPUR

① ② 11.05

CR

③ 11

⑫

12

DOWN MID KENT UP MID KENT

13

[SO 510] LBW S: LBSC

CM & EE Crossing

8.35 (9.75 Vic)

47 TRAMLINK

Platforms 1,2,3 ⑨ 4,5,6 ⑧

① ② ③ ④ ⑤ n

NORWOOD JUNCTION 8.55

Controlled from Three Bridges ASC (T)

② EDEN PARK 12.34

① ⑫

① ② WEST WICKHAM 13.19

14

① ⑫

LCH [SO 330] S:SE

East Croydon West Croydon

GULLET

8.67 n

14C: to West and East Croydon

② HAYES 14.34 ⑫

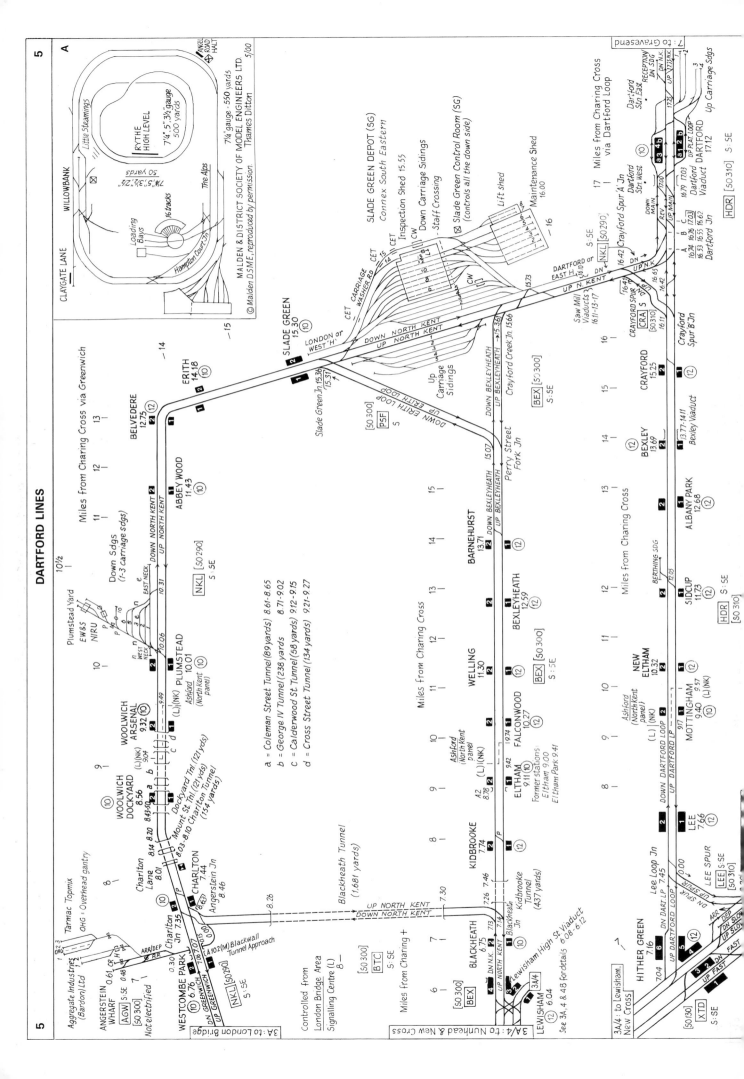

DARTFORD LINES

CHISLEHURST & SHORTLANDS - SEVENOAKS - (TONBRIDGE)

7 : to Maidstone East

7 : to Rochester

DN CHATHAM MN
DN CHATHAM MN

Down Sdgs A20(T)
18.23 18.67 19.24
18.60 Eynsford Tunnel (828 yds)
M25

(Lullingstone)
19.39 Eynsford Viaduct 19.73-79

EYNSFORD 20.32 ② ① ⑧

[50140] SBJ S: LCD
Controlled by Victoria (VS) P5B
(at Clapham Jn)

SWANLEY 17.31 ⑫
Swanley Jn. 17.46
17.37 17.50 17.78

DOWN MAIDSTONE
UP MAIDSTONE

23 24 25 MAIDSTONE

DOWN MAIDSTONE FAST
DOWN MAIDSTONE SLOW
25.06 25 — 25.60

OTFORD 24.06 ② ① ⑧
Otford GF 24.14
M26 24.53 Otford Jn 24.54

SHOREHAM (Kent) 22.52 ② ① ⑧

22½

— 26

THE GUSSET
2220 8 cars
DOWN QUARRY SDG
22.31 12 cars

DOWN BAT & BALL
UP BAT & BALL

BAT & BALL 25.51 ⑧
[50140] OJS S: LCD

VS/AD — 1

COM 10.21
19.92
1991

DOWN LOOP
UP LOOP
UP MAIN
SEVENOAKS 22.09 ⑫
Engr's —22.40
83 2S DM

9

21¾

DOWN MAIN
UP MAIN
DUNTON GREEN 2046 ② ① ⑫
20.24 R. Darent Bridge 2.06
M26 (12)

KNOCKHOLT 1644 ② ① ⑫
16.14 16.70
M25 17.20 18.58
18.68 Polhill Tunnel (1 mile. 851 yds)

CHELSFIELD 15.25 ② ① ⑫
1567 Chelsfield Tunnel (597 yards)

XTD [50130] S: SE
Controlled by Ashford (AD) SC

14.07

Miles from Charing Cross

ORPINGTON 13.65 ⑫
⑧ 7 ⑤ 6 ③ 4 ② 1
11 cars
Carriage Sdgs
1333 4 3 2 1
13.36
13.17

DOWN SLOW
UP SLOW
DOWN FAST
UP FAST

PETTS WOOD 12.53 ⑫
③ 4 ① 2

Petts Wood Jns [TLP2]
Ch.X (2.25) mean
Vic (1.31)
TONBRIDGE LP (3.33)

DOWN SLOW
UP SLOW
DN FAST
UP FAST

12.24 13.29 Vic
13.38

* Hawkwood Jn

* = Hawkwood Jn

[50130]
CSM 3
UP CH.L. 12.30
1169 1275 1166

ST MARY CRAY 14.57 ② ① ⑫
St Mary Cray Jns
Vic 13.17 mean
Ch.X 12.10
13.10 13.25

Cray Viaduct 15.06-15.10
12
[50110] VIR S: LCD

TLP1 [50130]
VAD UP FAST T.L.
REVERSIBLE LOOP
CHATHAM LOOP
[AD/VS]
1281
11.53 11.33
1215 12.15

BICKLEY 11.76 ⑧ VIR [50110] S: LCD
Bickley Jns
Bickley 12.40
12.49 DN FAST T.L.
12.38
12.07

CHISLEHURST 11.19 ⑫
XTD [50130] S: SE
CSM [50130]
④ ② 3 ① 1
CSM 2 UP CHATHAM LOOP

38: to Grove Park

S: SE [50130] CSM 1

BROMLEY SOUTH 10.71 ⑫
⑧ [50110] S: LCD
② 10.58
4: to Nunhead/Beckenham Junction

SHORTLANDS 10.03 ⑧
DOWN CHATHAM SLOW
UP CH SLOW
DOWN CHATHAM FAST
UP CHATHAM FAST
10.18
10.58

Miles from Victoria via Herne Hill

6A

22½ 22.46
22.40 22.53 Sevenoaks Tunnel (1 mile, 1693 yards)

[50130] XTD S: SE
Controlled by Ashford (AD) SC

2250

DOWN MAIN
UP MAIN

A21(T) 26.68 HILDENBOROUGH 2702 ⑫
① ② 27.02

10B: to Tonbridge

River Medway Bridge 28.76

23 24 25 26 27 28 29
Miles from Charing Cross

6

© Copyright Quail Map Company. No reproduction without permission

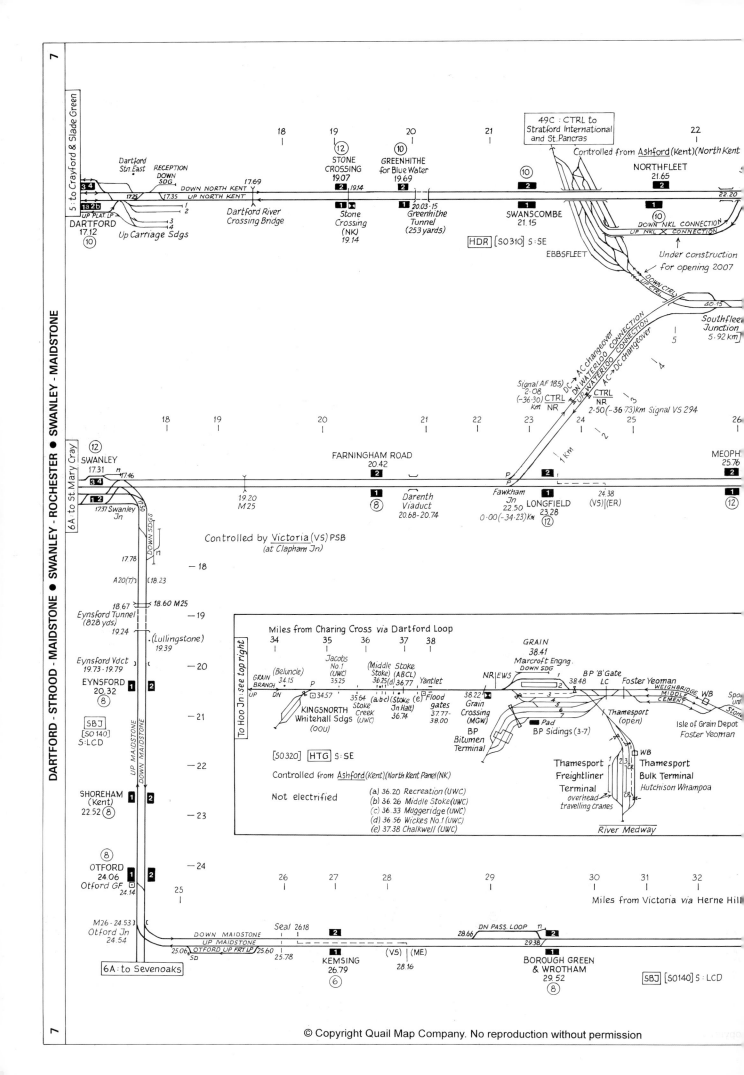

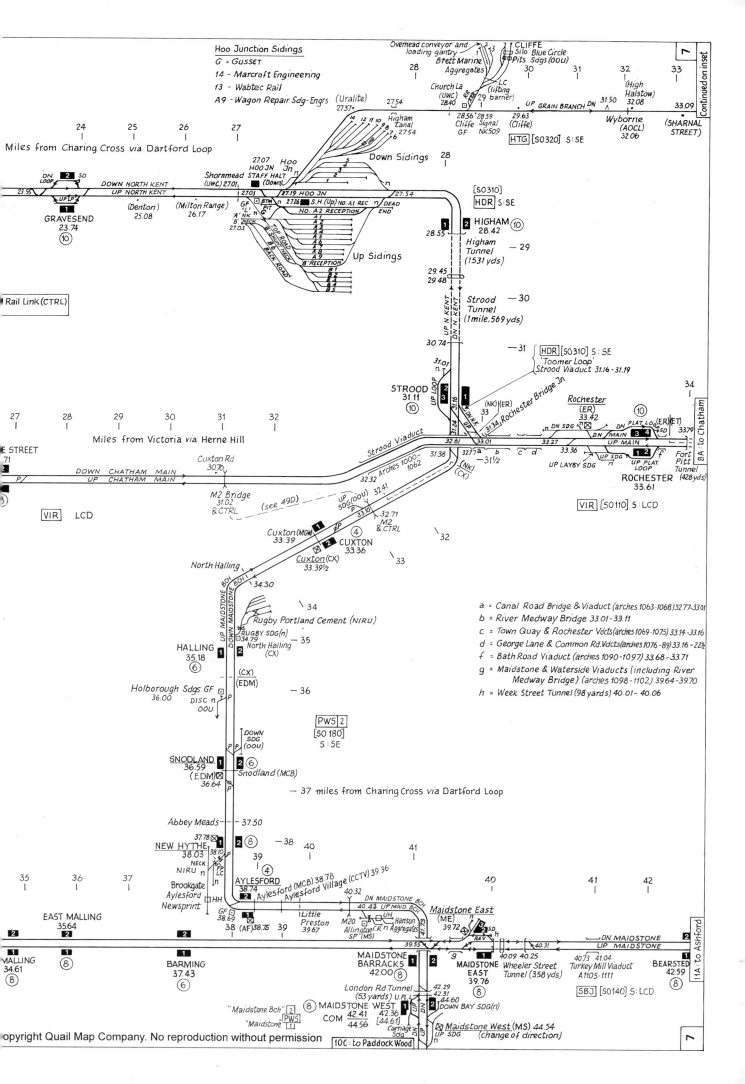

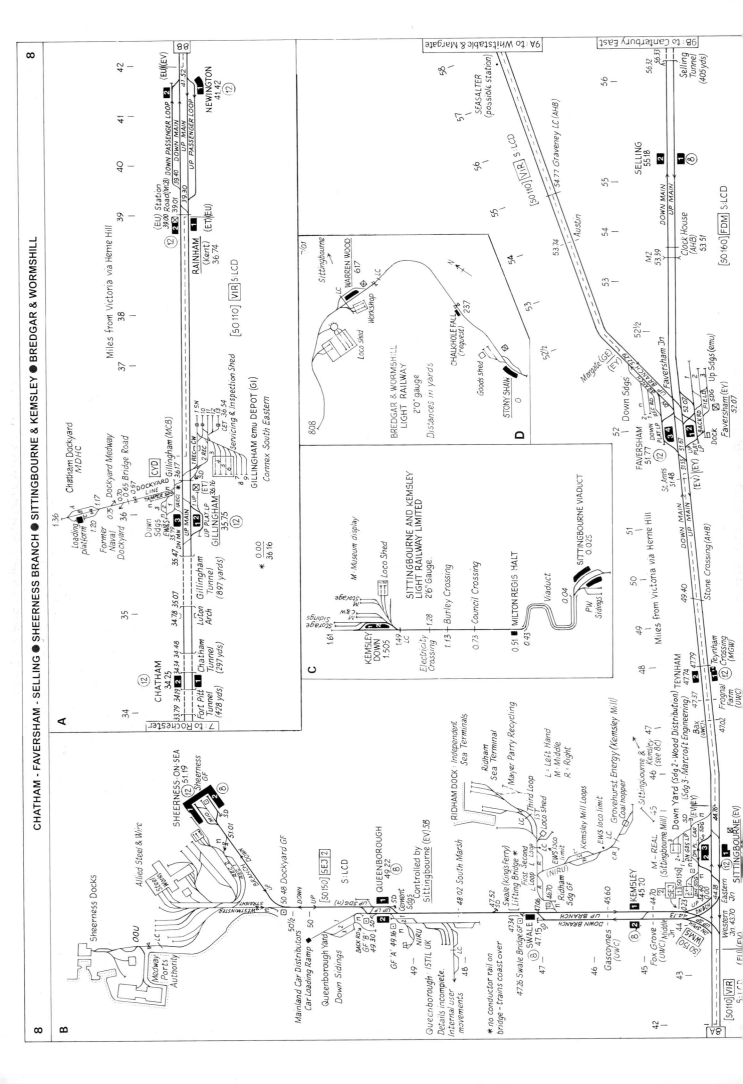

9

Miles from Victoria via Herne Hill

Miles from Charing Cross via Chelsfield & Canterbury West

MARGATE for Cliftonville 73.69 (12)
Margate OOU

BROADSTAIRS 77.09
S: LCD (Harbour Jn 77.60)
DUMPTON PARK 78.26
Ramsgate Viaduct 79.02

WESTGATE ON SEA 72.35 (12)
BIRCHINGTON ON SEA 70.56

RAMSGATE EMU DEPOT (RM) Connex South Eastern
EAST YARD
WEST YARD
Lifting Shed
Carriage Servicing Shed
Carriage Inspection Shed

RAMSGATE 85.67 [VIR] [ACR] COM 79.21
S: change of directions

HERNE BAY 62.58

CHESTFIELD & SWALECLIFFE 60.45 (12)

WHITSTABLE 59.06
58.63

[S011O] [VIR] S: LCD

Hoplands (Chislet Colly SB) 75.16
Port Farm 76.06
(CHISLET COLLIERY) Staff Halt 74.57
Grove Ferry (AHB) 76.62
Wall End 77.26
Sarre Bridge 78.37 Cater
Monkton Court 79.38 Mile Drove
Sheriffs Court 80.60
Walters Hall 80.44

[S022O] [ACR] S: SE

MINSTER 81.64
High St (8) [EBE] Minster East Jn 82.17
Minster West Jn 82.18
Sevenscore (AHB) 83.10
Cliffsend (AHB) 84.04
Ebbsfleet & Cliffsend Halt 83.41

[BME] Minster South Jn
[S024O]

DOWN MAIN / UP MAIN

Long Salts 85.07
Richborough Castle 84.48
Richborough (AHB) 85.24
Ash Road (AHB) 85.60
Woodnesborough (AHB) 86.12
SANDWICH (SW) 86.38 (8)
Sandwich 86.37
Blue Pigeon 87.46
Gore Top 88.69

North Wall (RG) 90.09
DEAL 90.56 (8)
Deal (EBZ) 90.43
Middle 90.42

Betteshanger Colliery (OOU) 89.11
Betteshanger Colliery (CLOSED)

CANTERBURY WEST 70.27 (8)
St. Dunstans 70.15
Former Oil Sdg 70.37
St. Stephens (CCTV)
Canterbury Vdct 61.27-23
Canterbury East 61.65 (8)
Whitehall (RG) 69.30
A2(T) 60.54
Chartham 67.14 (4)
Deaney 66.60
CHARTHAM
Chartham Hatch LC (AHB) 58.65
Broad Oak (AHB) 71.77
STURRY 72.58 (6)
Hoplands Farm 74.51
BEKESBOURNE 64.58 (8)
Bekesbourne Viaduct 64.66

Selling Tunnel (405 yds) 56.52 S: LCD

13: to Dover

BB: to Faversham
11B: to Ashford

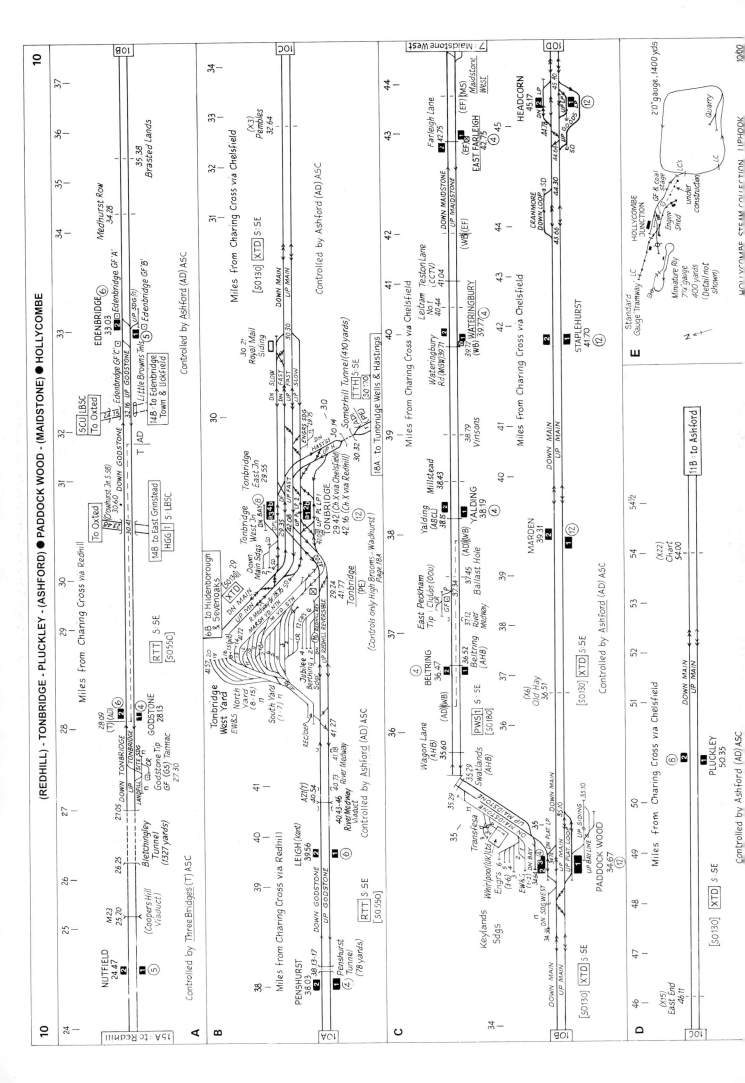

(MAIDSTONE) - ASHFORD - DOLLANDS MOOR ● ASHFORD - CHILHAM - (CANTERBURY)

A

Miles from Victoria via Herne Hill

56.56 (ME)(AD) 56.50

Hothfield
Tarmac Sdgs (n)
CR Hoppers(n) 55.70
REC 56.42
Beechbrook Farm
former station
(details on 51)

[SO140] [SB3] S:LCD

Controlled by Maidstone East (ME)

M20 55.00-06
CHARING 53.11 ⑥

50A: to London
M20 CTRL 43.77
—44.02—

50A: to Ashford Eurotnl

BEARSTED 42.59 ⑧

DOWN MAIDSTONE 48.60
UP MAIDSTONE

HOLLINGBOURNE 45.02 ⑥

HARRIETSHAM 47.36 ⑥

LENHAM 49.11

7: to Maidstone East

B

9B: to Canterbury West and Ramsgate

66

Chilham Road (MGW)
CHILHAM 65.09 ④
Chilham Mill (UWC)(R(G) 64.76

Miles from Charing Cross via Chelsfield
Buiting Grange Buckwell 61.38 61.70
61.64 Buiting
[SO220] ACR S:SE

WYE (MGW) 60.32 60.26
Wye (EBT)
(AD) (ABT)

Spring Grove 59.47

UP BRANCH
DOWN BRANCH
57.10 Down Yard East Jn 'G'
5773 (AD) (EBT)
M20 57.37

U = Rinser
v = CET (Controlled emission toilet discharge)
d = Wash down apron
t = Test pad
p = snowplough

Ashford PAD Sidings
Down Yard Carriage Sidings
ASHFORD INTERNATIONAL 56.12 [5919]
Charing + {56.21 (AF) 90.55km}
Ashford Viaducts (1430m)
Ashford Asc
CR

Godinton Rd/ Ashford Trnl (254m)
DN CTRL UP CTRL
cut & cover

MAIDSTONE RELIEF LP
DOWN WEST CHORD
UP WEST CHORD

Ashford 'B' Jn 58 61(via Maidstone) 55 54(via Tonbridge)
Ashford 'C' Jn 56.02
Beaver Ashford Road 56.04
Ashford 'D' Jn

Miles from Charing Cross via Chelsfield

58

Sevington Sidings
EWS- Balfour Beatty
SEVINGTON LOOP 57.64

Ashford Willes-borough
Ashford East
Crane Repair Depot
East Berthing Sdgs
Newtown Berthing Sdgs
DOWN HASTINGS
UP HASTINGS
[SO 200] ATH S:SE

Harringe 61.60 61.65

A20 62.64

(Racecourse)⑧ 63.73
WESTENHANGER 64.15

A20 64.40 64.76 64.55 -65.0)

Sandling Tunnel (100 yards)
SANDLING 65.36 65.01
Sandling Tunnel (954 yards) 65.58

C

Miles from Charing Cross via Chelsfield

Dollands Moor see 50D
Dollands overhead Moor limit E.Jn 66.40
Saltwood Tunnel (954 yards) 66.27 66.21
(Cheriton Jn) 68.0
Dover Line Vdct (176m)
Saltwood Junctions 66.38 66.31 66.40 66.25 66.36
DOWN DOVER
UP DOVER 67.09 68.20

[SO130] XTD S:SE

13: to Dover

18D: to Rye & Hastings

50C: to London
XTD [SO130]
DOWN MAIN
UP MAIN
Ashford 'A' Jn 58.78 58.33
Maidstone East 56.56 (ME)(AD)

CHART LEACON
T & RS MD (AF)
Bombardier Transportation
CLA 8 Roads 1-9
CLA 9 Roads 10-18

Test Shop Repair Shop
STORES

Platforms ⑫ 5/6 (a-b-c)56.08-56.22
⑱ 4/3 (90-13)56.02-56.23(90-54CR)
⑫ 2/1 (a-b-c)56.02-56.16
1/2 3rd rail
3/4 3rd rail & OHLE
5/6 3rd rail
(OHLE to E.end only)

(d) DOWN CANTERBURY
(e) UP CANTERBURY
(f) DOWN CTRL CHORD
(g) UP CTRL CHORD
(h) DOWN FAST
(j) UP FAST
(k) DOWN SLOW
(l) UP SLOW
(o) OHLE limit

IOD: to Tonbridge

© Copyright Quail Map Company. No reproduction without permission

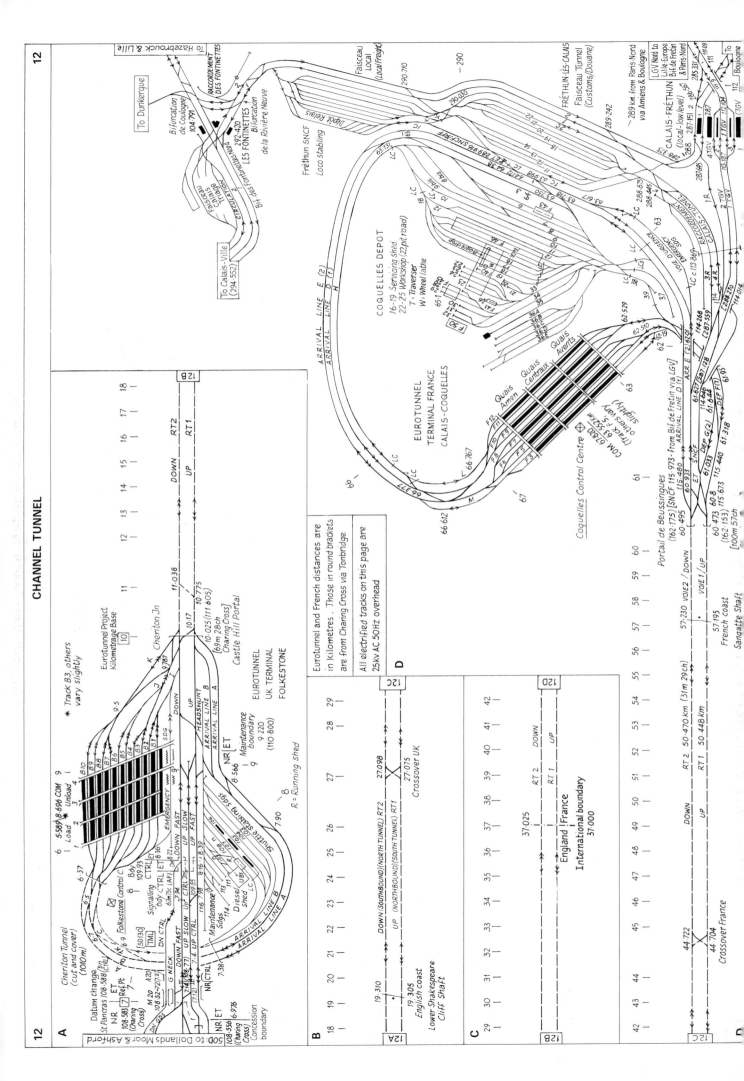

CHANNEL TUNNEL

(CANTERBURY) & (DEAL) - DOVER ● FOLKESTONE - DOVER ● KENT & EAST SUSSEX RAILWAY ● EAST KENT RAILWAY

—91

WALMER 92.27 2
⑧
92.54 1

Cold Blow (R/G)
Deal
(EB2)
(YE)

—92

DOWN DEAL
UP DEAL

—93

[50.240] BME
S: SE & LCD Jt

MARTIN MILL
for St.Margarets Bay 95.05
⑧ 2

—94

95 miles from Charing Cross
via Chelsfield & Canterbury West

Deal
(EB2)
(YE)

96.25
9660
Guston Tunnel
(1412 yards)
9744

—96

—97

—98 —99

Chariton Tunnel (265 yards)

Priory Tunnel (158 yards) platforms

DOVER PRIORY ⑧ ⑩ ⑫
7726 (via Canterbury)
7723 (via Ashford)
UP CHATHAM A20 (M)
7732 DN CHATHAM
DN Dover Harbour Tunnel (684 yards)

Carriage
Sdgs

Line description change 7762 77.651
DOWN MAIN UP MAIN

77.76 —76.53
COM 0.14—76.53
S: SE H5E
[50130]

● (Hawkesbury Street Junction)

(Archcliffe Junction)

76.36
7654 (Old Pilot Tower)

Sea Defence Wall

© Copyright Quail Map Company. No reproduction without permission

former
Tilmanstone
Colliery

1360 boundary
Eastry EAST KENT LIGHT RAILWAY
EKR LC
EYTHORNE
73.24
Golgotha Tunnel 72.10—72.31
(477 yards)
LC 0.75/71.75
LC 0.72
0.66
71.46

Former BR
connection

Shepherds Well (SH)
71.51
SHEPHERDS WELL
71.60
⑧

SHEPHERDS WELL
0.55
71.66

NR/EKR
3

LONG SDG
UP SDG

Lydden Tunnel
(1mile, 609 yds)

73.14

74

Kearsney Viaduct 74.78

KEARSNEY
75.09
⑧ 2

(SH) (YE)

(SH)
(YE)

—75

—76

DOWN MAIN
UP MAIN

DOWN CHAT
UP CHATHAM

76.32
Buckland Jn

99.05

76.77
76.65

[50160] FDM
[50130/160]
S: LCD

77.08
77.16

Carriage
Sdgs 3

2 2.3 1

70 miles from Victoria via Herne Hill

71

72

70.56 Soles Farm

Snowdown (00U)
6973 1
6977 2
SNOWDOWN
67.90
⑧

70.28

AYLESHAM
68.66 2
⑧ 1
67.60
ADISHAM
67.60
⑧ 1

[50160] FDM S: LCD

Three Arch
Viaduct
67.35

65 66 67 68 69

DOWN MAIN
UP MAIN

Rother
Bridge
[58.59]
5.63

NORTHIAM (NM)
6.55
[59.51]
(7.00)
2 LOOP [59.47]
6.51
MKT

(A28)

6

—KENT AND EAST SUSSEX RAILWAY—
THE TENTERDEN RAILWAY COMPANY LIMITED

A   Locations are related to telephone
poles. WM signal box is at TP105

Three sets of mileages are shown
Different mileages appear in different publications
All mileages have been calculated from a
survey conducted by B.R. in 1948
Unbracketed mileages from zero at Tenterden
Square bracketed mileages from zero at
Charing Cross via Headcorn
Round bracketed mileages from mean zero
at Robertsbridge

WITTERSHAM ROAD (WM) repositioned
[5720] (9.3)
Wittersham
Bank
4.20
4.2b Engrs Sdg GF
[5722]

Z: open ended for
vehicle deliveries

NB Station
reposstioned

Hexden
Bridge
5.06
[58.02]

Newmill
Bridge
3.20
[56.16]

10.18
P.W. Depot
BACK A
ROAD B D

BODIAM (BM)
10.20
[63.15]
(3.35)

[63.13]

DOWN UP

DOWN UP

(Dixter Halt)
c 8.11

DOWN UP

5 4 3 2

10 9 8 7

1 1 1

B : Back Road
D : Pullman Dock
E : End Siding

Bogie
storage

E 0.00

Carriage
Works

D

TENTERDEN TOWN
0.15
[53.11]
(13.40)

(TN)

5/02

Tenterden Bank

Cranbrook Rd
0.63
[53.59]

063
[53.59]

ORPINS
1.56 [54.32]
1.46
CR
Sewage
Works
Sdg
1.48 ORPINS
SDG

ROLVENDEN (RN)
[54.42] (12.06)

KSU

L.S & Works
* The only visible M.P. is ¹/₂
which would make Rolvenden
1.42 (LC 1.39) with adjustments to east & west

3

1 2

Shepherds Well (SH) (YE)
71.51
71.60
⑧

UP SDG
NORTHIAM
(NM)
[59.51]
(7.00)
2 1

Miles from Charing Cross via Chelsfield

(Warren Staff Halt)

(Warren Staff Halt)
72.02

Folkestone East Jns (A&B)
7070 70.97 71.01
7072 (A) (YE)
Passenger
Sdgs

FFH 1

Martello Tunnel
(533 yds)

71.22
71.08 * 1

71.47
Train Roads
71.22 (14 cars)
Berthing Sdgs 3
(NIRU) (14 cars)

[50230] S: SE

* Mileage reversal

FOLKESTONE EAST Staff Halts

Folkestone
(AD) (YE)
Folkestone Viaduct
7072 (A) 7027 70.39
(Arches)
1134—1152)
71.34 71.63 71.62

FOLKESTONE CENTRAL
70.27 70.39
[50130]
XTD S: SE
(AD) (YE)

71.08 DN FOLKESTONE HARB
7123
DN FOLK. HARB
LC (MB)
Folly
Road (CCTV)
71.29

Radnor Vdct
OOU

Swing Bridge (former)
1154—1135)

Harbour Vdct (Arches)
71.54 NIRU

FOLKESTONE WEST
6922
⑧ 1
[50130]
XTD S: SE

DOWN DOVER
UP DOVER

FOLKESTONE HARBOUR

6973
(EBB) closed
(12)
72.07 72.02 71.71 71.63 71.62
S/crossing 1
72.25
Roll on Pier 71.18
Roll-off

75

Trip wire alarm (down side)

DOWN MAIN
UP MAIN

(SHAKESPEARE
Staff Halt)
75.09

(SHAKESPEARE Staff Halt)
75.14

Shakespeare Tunnel
(1387 yards)
75.77

74

73

Abbotscliffe Tunnel
(1mile, 182 yards)
73.23 74.31

72

71

70

69

IIC 8.500 to Sandling & Ashford

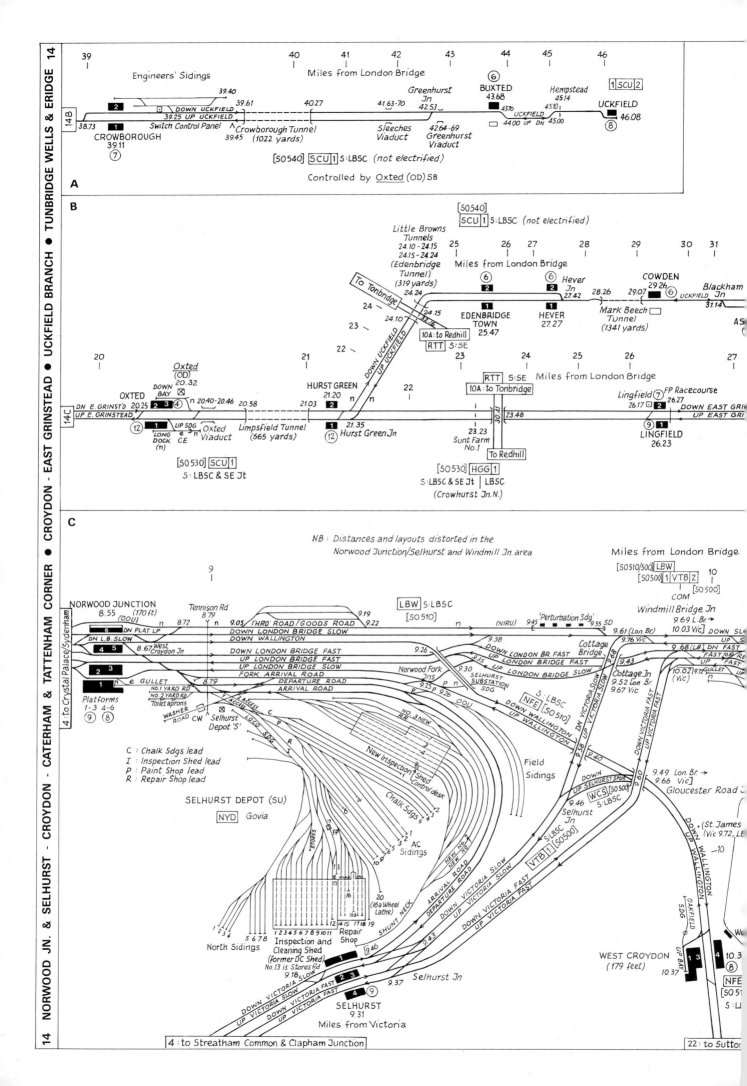

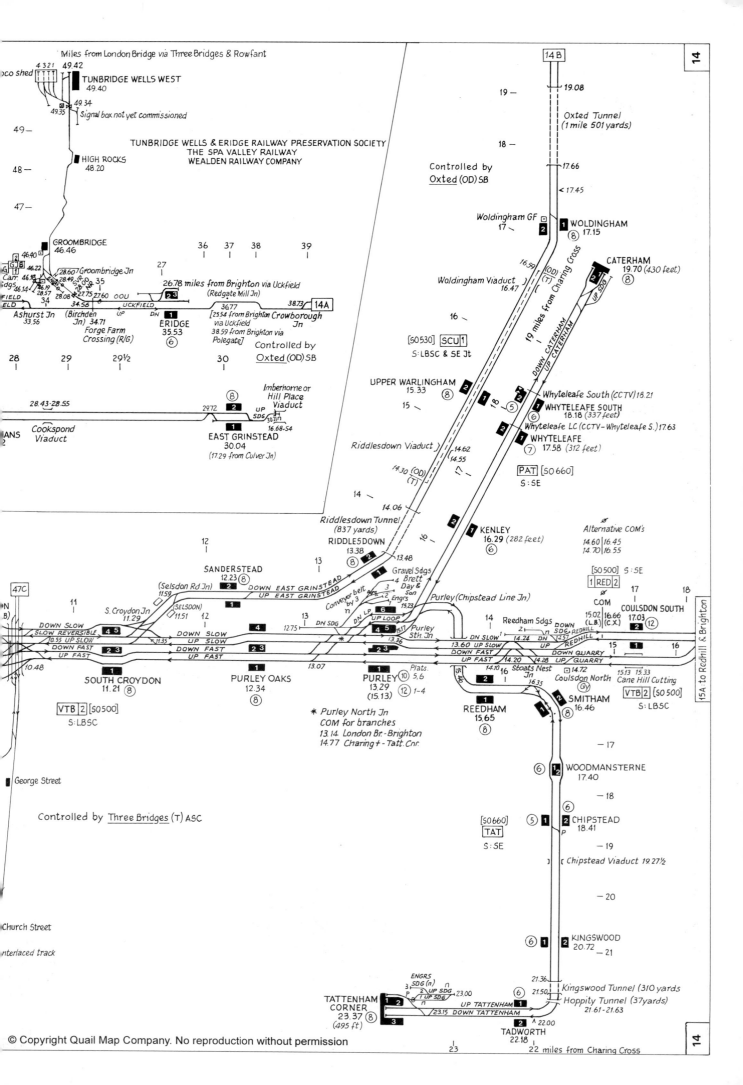

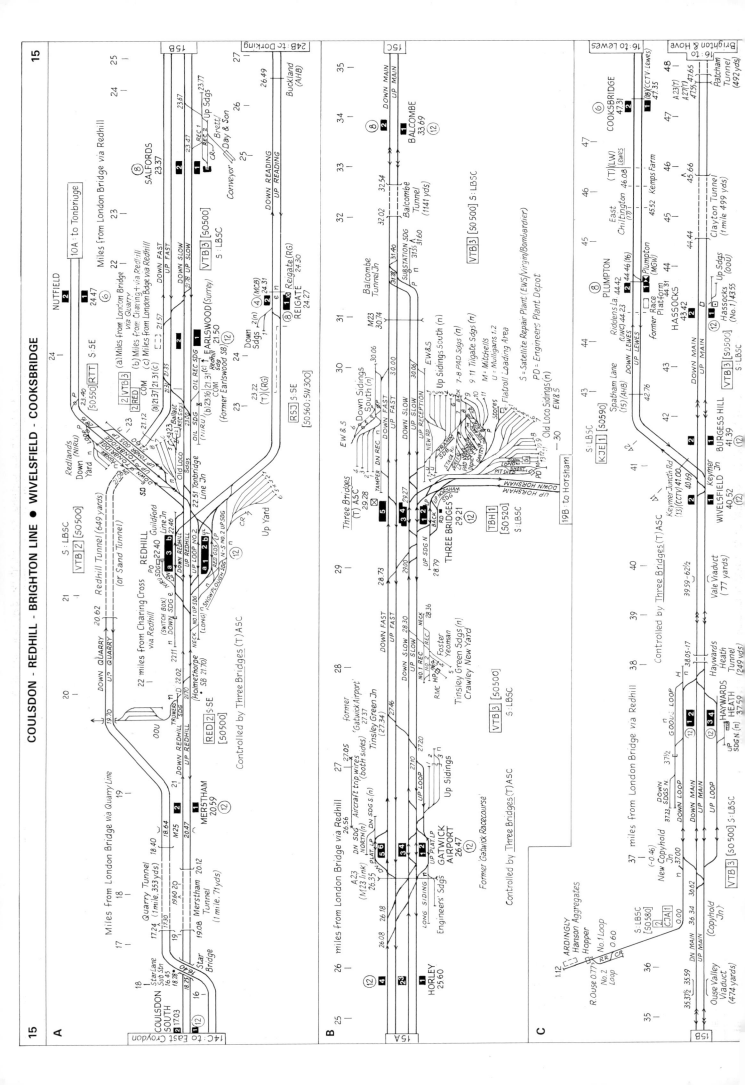

COULSDON - REDHILL - BRIGHTON LINE ● WIVELSFIELD - COOKSBRIDGE

BRIGHTON - HOVE, PRESTON PARK & LEWES ● VOLK'S ELECTRIC RAILWAY

17A: to Newhaven & Eastbourne

THE LAVENDER LINE
c ¾ mile of track in use

Lavender
Line
Preservation
Society

14.28 Dingley Dell
Not
confirmed
by operator

— 14

13.75 — crossing

Dock   ISFIELD
Ramp   13.48
1 2   13.45
3
LC

A

Lewes Jn
Down Lewes Sdgs GF
50.03/8.03
Up Sdg
Lewes (LW)
50.03/8.03
8

Lewes Platforms
1,2 (12)
3,4 (7)
5   (8)

— 48.49 Hamsey River
48
49

DOWN LEWES 49.49
4967
UP LEWES
Lewes Tunnel
(395 yards)
49.74 LEWES 777
713
718

[8] CCTV-Lewes]
Hamsey (19)   47.35
(AHB) 48.12

KJE1 [S:0590]
S:LBSC

COOKSBRIDGE
47.31 (6)

Kingston Tunnel (107 yards)
A27(T) 6.50
(T)(LW)

— 49

PRESTON PARK
49.21 (12)

Preston Park Jn
49.43

Controlled by Three Bridges (T) ASC

VTB3 [S0500]
S:LBSC

BTL [SO62G]
S:LBSC

Falmer Tunnel (490 yards)
FALMER
3.39   3.62
4.05
(7) 2

Hodshrove Viaduct 2.20-2.24
MOULSECOOMB
1.56

DOWN EAST BRANCH
UP EAST BRANCH
(Kemp Town Jn)
0.66
0.63 Ditchling Road Tunnel (63 yards)
LONDON ROAD (Brighton)
0.57

London Road Viaduct
(390 yards)

0.44
(7) 2

Patcham Tunnel
(492 yards)
47.65
48.07

3.2.1
OOU
UP MAIN DOWN MAIN
UP LOOP
49.35

49.73 Dyke Road

Top Yard
Down Sdgs(n)
(NIRU)

— 50

0.26
0.23 (Goods Incline)
0.31 Montpelier Jn 0.14

VTB3
[50500]
S:LBSC

Brighton 'Loco Works'
(former Pullman
Car Co's w/shop)
oou/closed
49.56

Cliftonville
Tunnel
(535 yards)
50.00

Govia

BRIGHTON
T & RSMD
(B)
Roads 6-12
in shed(n)

Lovers Walk

BPJ
49.74

DOWN CLIFTONVILLE SPUR
UP CLIFTONVILLE SPUR

[50630]
PPH
S:LBSC

WASHER RD

SDGS 2
SDGS 1
SN No.1
49.65 CWL

SHUNT NECK (n)
LOCO GOODS REC/DEP (n)
CARRIAGE ROAD

CARRIAGE ROAD NORTH
NORTH SDG No.1
SN LOVERS WK NO.1
4975
5000

ENGINEERS' SDG
RELEASE

MONTPELIER
W.CARR RD
CARR RD STH
LWZ
LW1
LW

MONTPELIER WEST LP

50.49 50.50
0.00 VTB3 BTL 0.00 (-0.04)
1 2 3   4-8
BLI1 (12) (8) (4)

BRIGHTON
Platforms
1 2 3 4 5 6 7 8

50.48

Lovers Walk
Inspection &
Cleaning Shed

Depot
Sdgs
e

Wall
Sdgs

Hove Tunnel
(220 yds)

0.40
(Holland Rd)
0.75

0.30
Hove

Hove Jn

BLI1 [50630]
S:LBSC

1.08

50.18
DOWN WEST BRANCH
UP WEST BRANCH

Hove Yard

50.48
50.38
50.48/e
1.18
1.23
1.28

[50.78] NO.1 UP SDG/e
0.SDG UP BTN
DOWN BTN
1.57

n NO.1 UP
UP LOOP
NO.2 UP SDG/e

1 2
3 HOVE
(50.56) 1.28
(12)

1.47

1.35

* Brighton West Coast Jn 0.05/50.42
B = Breakdown Crane
LW 3 (Lovers Walk No.3) Snow & Ice

* Brighton West Coast Jn 0.05/50.42

20A: to Worthing

Volks Level Crossings
(A) = Double yellow flashing lights
(B) = Double yellow flashing lights,
      gated on landward side

VOLK'S ELECTRIC RAILWAY
(Brighton & Hove City Council)
Gauge: 2'8½" (825mm). Electrified 110V d.c., third-rail
□ Workshop & power plant

PASTON PLACE
(½-WAY)

LC(A) 0.44
LC(B) LC(B)
Banjo Groyne

AQUARIUM
0.00
viaduct

Car Shed

Brighton Beach

LC LC LC LC LC LC LC LC LC LC LC LC LC LC

MARINA (BLACK ROCK)
1.05

A

To: Lewes
8.08
50.08

[50590] S: LBSC

KJE 3

Lewes Short Mile 50.29-50.40/8.29-8.40 (Lewes East Jn)

8.52
50.65/50.75
A2m
9 —

Southerham Bridge (River Ouse)
50.64 Southerham
50.69 Southerham
51 —

Southerham Jn. 51.11/9.11
9 —
Ends Cow
Lane No.1
9.30

Beddingham (20)/(AHB)
9.79 10.08
10 —

Lewes (LW)(BK)

DOWN MAIN
UP MAIN

Glynde Reach Viaduct
52.20
53 —

52.59 Asheham

53.36 Itford/R/G Lewes
53.40 SOUTHEASE
(CCO)
(LW) Lewes

GLYNDE
11.14

Loover Barn
11.62

11 —

12.42 Lower Barn No.1
12 —

Ripe (21)/(AHB)
13.25
13 —

13.56 Firle Crossing

Selmeston (22)/(AHB)
14.58
14 —

15 —

Berwick (BK) 15.55
Berwick (23)
BERWICK (8)
15.50
16 —

Miles from Brighton

[50590] KJE 3 S: LBSC

Dukes 18.72
17.29 Wilmington (25)/(AHB)
(BK)(PG) DOWN MAIN
17 — 18 — 19 —

Polegate 19.42
1935 (PG)(CDB)
Polegate Crossing (PG) (26)
19.34

former (Polegate Jn)
1960 ● 1968 former direct line
UP MAIN
—20 20.65 Harmers
21 —

21.39 21.75
HAMPDEN PARK (8)

Mountfield Road (MCB)(76)
21.71 Hampden Park(CDB)
—22

former (Stonecross Jn) 21.41 DN BEXHILL
2 miles reverse to Willingdon Jn

20.36 Willingdon Jn
from Brighton via Stonecross Jn
—23

20.57 Winkney No.1
20.70 Winkney No.2

[50600] WJB S: LBSC
A2m 6
Pevensey (CCV) 23.03
LC2301
(CCV)(CDB)
UP SDG 1 Engr's n
UP BX
PEVENSEY AND
WESTHAM 23.07
23 —
17B

DOWN MAIN
UP MAIN

[50590] KJE 3 S: LBSC
Hampden Park (CDB)
(CDB)(EB)
23.15
23.34
23.59 Eastbourne (EB)
EASTBOURNE 23.73
(12) 1 2 3
No.1
506
23.30 CW
CARRIAGE CLEANING
ENGINEER'S n
506
Exmover machine
(Gv)

B

PEVENSEY BAY 23.68
2
Wallsend (28)(CCTV) 23.72
4

DOWN BEXHILL
UP BEXHILL

NORMANS BAY 25.77
4 2
Havensmouth
Pevensey Sluice (29)/(AHB) 26.59
26.00 Mills
(CCV)(CCW)

Beach

27 —

COODEN BEACH 27.53
2 1 6

COLLINGTON 29.04
2 1 4

Bexhill (CCW) 29.61
2
29.69
29.77
BEXHILL 29.69
(12)
29 — 30 —

WJB [50600] S: LBSC

OOU(n)
Galley Hill GF 30.60
31 —

32 miles from Brighton (direct)

St Leonards Inspection Shed
Carriage Shed
St Leonards (WEST MARINA)
St Leonards Railway Engineering (SE)
STORES SDG
RECEPTION ROAD
32.56
32.70
DOWN BEXHILL
UP BEXHILL

Bo-Peep Jn(BJ)
60.69 (BJ)(EDL) 60.65
60.71
Bo-Peep Tunnel (1318yds)
32.78 Bo-Peep Jn
[50170]
[50600] TTH
S: SE

18C: to Hastings
18C: to Tonbridge
CW

C

ALDERNEY RAILWAY

Breakwater
0.0
--- tracks concreted over
Inner Harbour
operational limit
Crabby Road LC 0.56
Brave Rd BRAVE ROAD 0.66 0.68
Fort Grosnez
School (foot) 0.77
Battery 1.27
Golf Club (foot) 1.39
Whitegates 1.72
Sharp's Farm 2.16
Corblets Rd 2.30
Berry's Crossing (foot) 2.38
MANNEZ QUARRY 2.54
2.57
Miniature Railway

All level crossings are 'open'

0   ¼   ½ mile

G = States of Guernsey
A = Alderney Rly Society
11/00
Standard gauge
Alderney Railway Society

D

ALDERNEY MINIATURE RAILWAY
7¼ gauge
440 yards

Pond
Ballast Siding
2001

NEWHAVEN:
Newhaven Town Yard (OOU)
EW&S
Car ramps
North Quay
Wharf Rd GF(OOU)
57.78N
Newhaven Harbour Jn
Newhaven Town (30)
56.58
56.67
56.55
56.25 57
NEWHAVEN TOWN
NEWHAVEN HARBOUR 56.51
(2)
NEWHAVEN MARINE 56.67
Beach Rd 57.38
Bishopstone Beach
BISHOPSTONE 58.03
[5TS] [50610] S: LBSC
SEAFORD SINGLE
UP DOWN
SEAFORD 58.77
(12)
58 miles from London Bridge via Redhill
57.31 RT/Harbour boundary

NHB [50610] S: LBSC
[NHB] [50610]

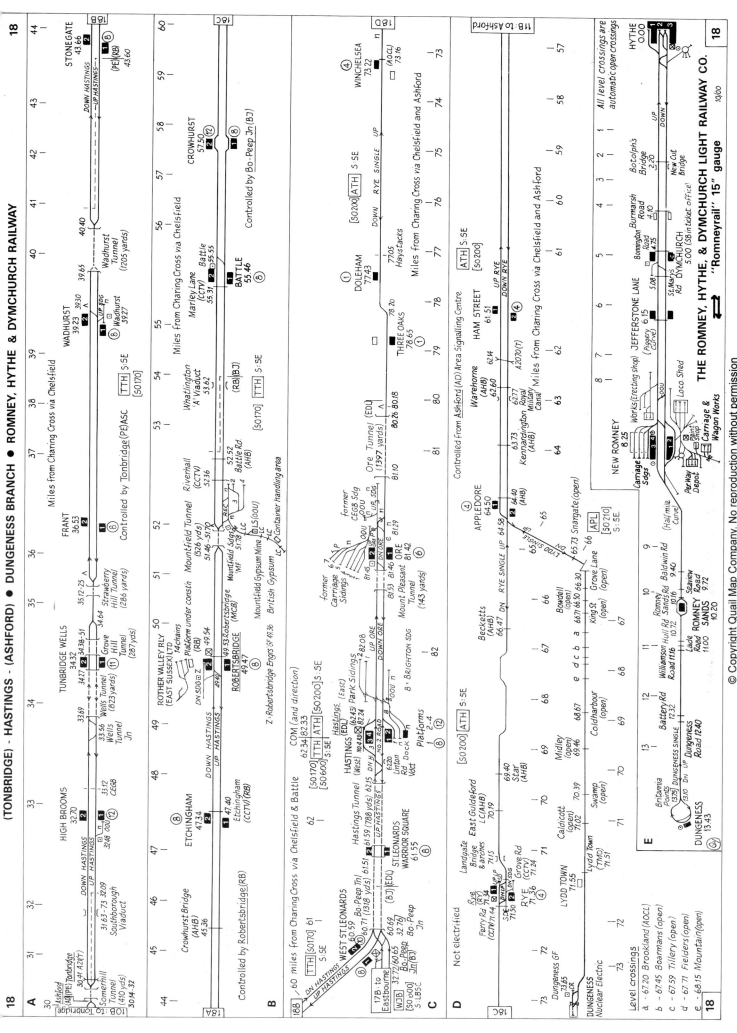

THE ROMNEY, HYTHE, & DYMCHURCH LIGHT RAILWAY CO.

"Romneyrail" 15" gauge

10/00

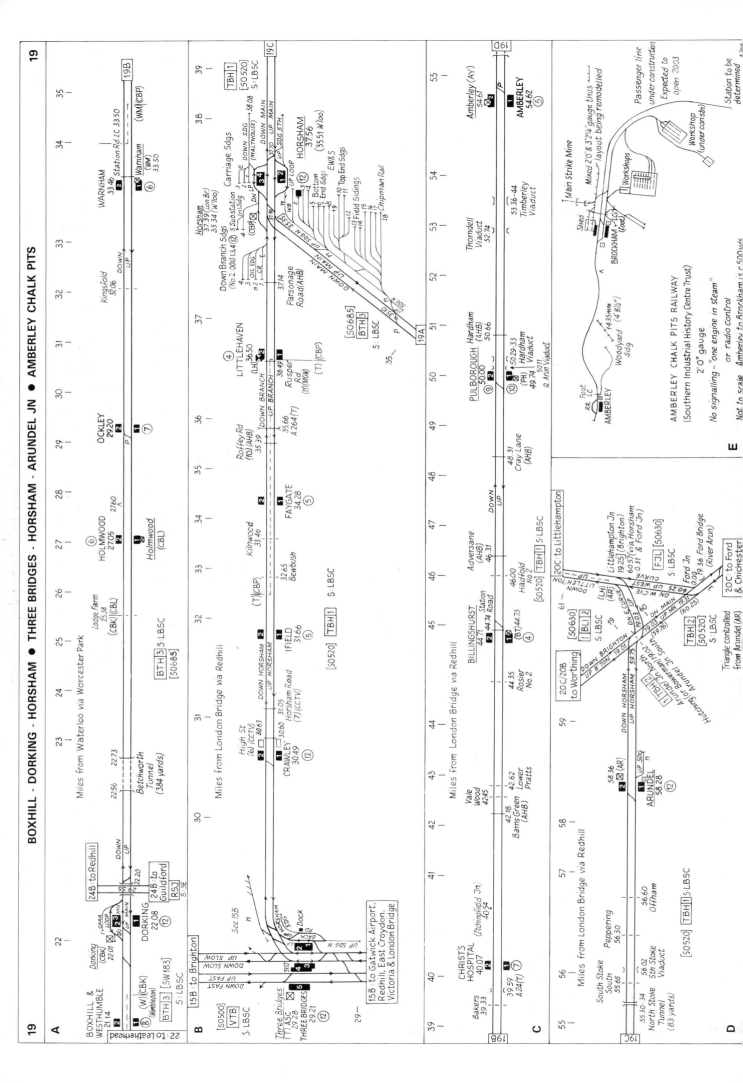

BOXHILL - DORKING - HORSHAM ● THREE BRIDGES - HORSHAM - ARUNDEL JN ● AMBERLEY CHALK PITS

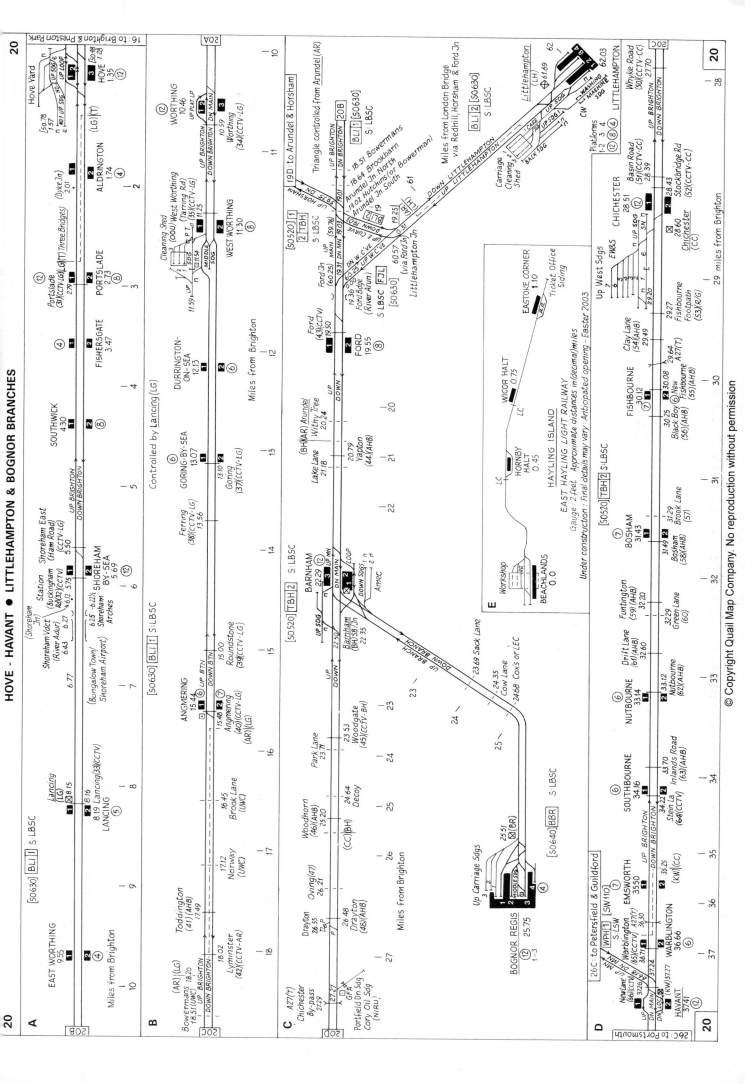

HOVE - HAVANT ● LITTLEHAMPTON & BOGNOR BRANCHES

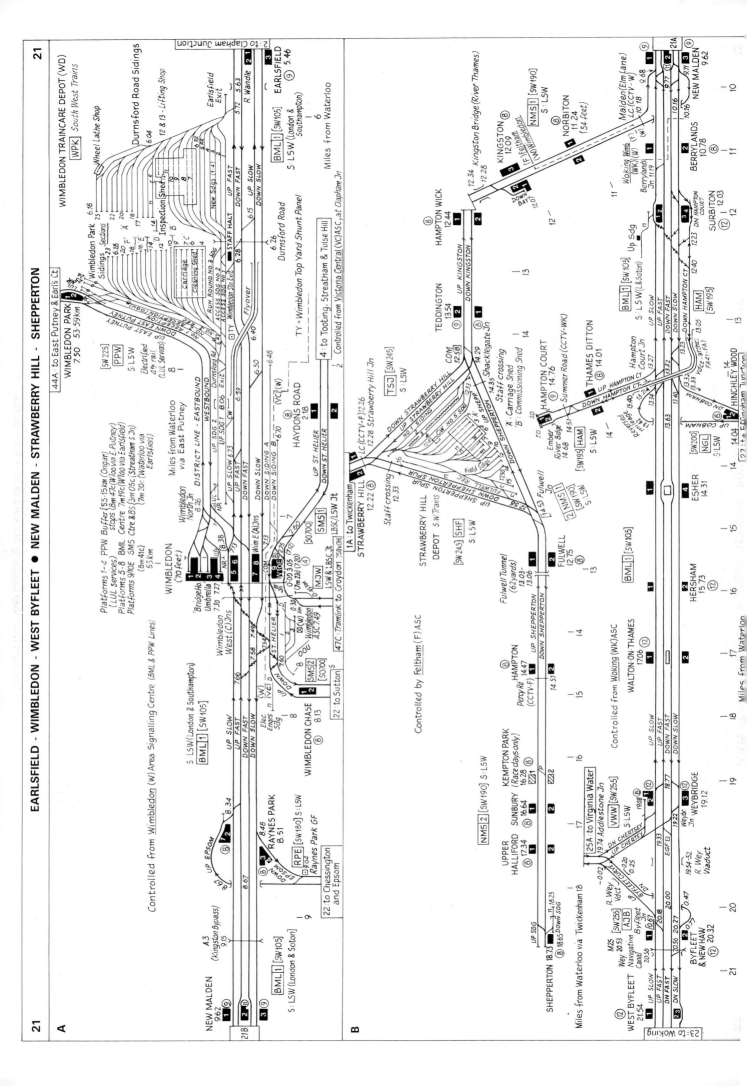

WIMBLEDOUN - EFFINGHAM JN./WEST CROYDON - BOXHILL AND ASSOCIATED LINES

21A: to Haydons Rd & Earlsfield

see also 21A

WIMBLEDON 7.19
LU

'Bridge Ho. Umbrella' 7.19

Wimbledon East(A)Jns

Dundonald Road
Merton Park
Morden Road
Phipps Bridge
Belgrave Walk
Mitcham

MJW S:LBSC

TRAMLINK - detail on 47C

East Fields Rd

4: to Tulse Hill

Wimbledon (C)Jns

Wimbledon ASC 7.49

Raynes Park Wimbledon Jn 9.04

SOUTH MERTON 8.61

MORDEN SOUTH 9.32

ST HELIER 9.69

WIMBLEDON CHASE 8.13

MITCHAM JUNCTION 10.30

BTH1 S0680 S:LBSC

DOWN PORTSMTH

UP PORTSMTH 9.19

Controlled by Victoria
ASC (VC) (at Clapham Jn)

HACKBRIDGE 11.41

CARSHALTON 12.30

CARSHALTON BEECHES

WALLINGTON 13.05

Beddington Lane
Therapia Lane
Ampere Way
Waddon Marsh
Wardle Park
WADDON 11.40
WEST CROYDON 10.35

Controlled by Three Bridges(T)ASC

14C: to Norwood Jn & Selhurst

Miles from London Bridge via Streatham

Miles from London Bridge via Forest Hill

Miles from London Bridge via West Croydon

RAYNES PARK

SUTTON COMMON 10.67

SUTTON 12.50

WEST SUTTON 11.47

CHEAM 15.76

BELMONT 16.01

BANSTEAD 17.40

EPSOM DOWNS 18.57 (350 feet)

EWELL EAST 17.27

EWELL WEST 12.78

STONELEIGH 11.74

WORCESTER PARK 10.53 (70 feet)

MOTSPUR PARK 10.11

MALDEN MANOR 9.64

TOLWORTH 12.06

CHESSINGTON NORTH 13.25

CHESSINGTON SOUTH 13.73

NEW MALDEN 9.62

BERRYLANDS 10.78

SURBITON 12.03

Berrylands Jn 11.19

Woking (WK) (W)

21B: to Teddington/Malden (Elm Lane)

Hampton Court Jn

21B: to Hampton Court

21B: to Esher & Weybridge

HINCHLEY WOOD 14.04

CLAYGATE 15.11

OXSHOTT 16.79

COBHAM & STOKE D'ABERNON 18.63

BOOKHAM 20.45

EFFINGHAM JN 21.10

Bethells 21.20

23: to Guildford

Controlled from Guildford (GD)ASC

Controlled from Woking (WK)ASC

Controlled from Wimbledon (W)ASC

ASHTEAD 16.19

LEATHERHEAD 18.02

BOXHILL & WESTHUMBLE 21.14

R. Mole Vdct. 18.29

Mickleham Tunnel (524 yards) 19.78

River Mole, Four Arch Jn 20.69

19A: to Dorking & Horsham

EPSOM 14.18

EPSOM DOWNS SINGLE

Miles from Waterloo

Miles from Waterloo via Worcester Park

Miles from Waterloo via Guildford

Miles from London Bridge via West Croydon

WEST BYFLEET - WOKING - GUILDFORD ● EFFINGHAM JN - GUILDFORD - ASH

21B: to Weybridge & Surbiton
22: to Surbiton
22: to Leatherhead

[22.15]

EFFINGHAM JUNCTION
1 21.04
2
21.10
Carriage Shed
(OOU)
72.113
21.27
DN SDG
21.38

⑧

UP SLOW
UP FAST
DOWN FAST
DOWN SLOW

WEST BYFLEET
21.54
1
⑫

HORSLEY
22.12
⑥
1

— 22

— 23

[SW105] [BML] 1 S·LSW (London & Southampton)

2365
2400
2370

East End Sdg
(WK) Woking ASC

24.20
(WK) Woking ASC

[SW200]
NGL
S·LSW

CLANDON
25.26
⑧
2 GSP 25.20

● Merrow

UP COBHAM
DOWN COBHAM

Miles from Waterloo via Cobham

KNAPHILL
● Woking Miniature Railway
(See inset below)

[SW105] [BML] 1 S·LSW

Controlled from Woking (WK) ASC

UP SLOW
UP FAST
DOWN FAST
DOWN SLOW

BROOKWOOD
27.79
1
⑫
2
EGSP

PEN
ROAD
⑫ (P6 ⑥)
WOKING
24.27
1
2 4 3
6 5

EW&S

Woking
Up Yard
[WKG 9]

Woking
Down Yard : EW&S
[WKG 8]

Redland Aggregates
Day Aggregates
Balfour Beatty

Pirbright Jn (29.39 mean)
29.31
29.30
29.48
29.49
2360
[SW120] — 30
[PAA] 1
S·LSW
DOWN ALTON
UP ALTON

Miles from Charing Cross 49
via Redhill

GUILDFORD NEW LINE JN
Guildford North Jn

LONDON ROAD (Guildford)
28.47
⑧
2

London Rd Vdct

WORPLESDON
26.65
1
2
[SW110]
[WPH] 1
S·LSW

UP GUILDFORD
DOWN GUILDFORD
Woking Jn
25.12
25.05
25.00

(WK)
(GD)
Area Signalling Centre
(GD) Area Signalling Centre

Controlled from Guildford

NORTH BOX SDGS
DN SDS SDG
29.82
30.02 29.77

UP MAIN
DOWN MAIN
DOWN MAIN
UP MAIN

— 30 (via Woking)
29.23 29.26
30.27 (via Woking; mileage reversal at 30.20 to [GTW])
+30.20 (Woking end) 29.70 (via Cobham)

GUILDFORD
GTW1 WPH1 NGL
(a) 30.35   30.05
(b)   30.07 29.52
(c)   30.14 29.59

Platforms 2-8 designated London End
Platforms 2-8 designated Portsmouth End

1
2 COB
3 COB
4
5 ASH
6
7 ASH
8 DOWN
3 2 1

30.40 (GD) ASC
30.43
Chalk Tunnel (845 yards)

UP MAIN
DN MAIN
UP MAIN

Carriage Sdgs
TAMPER
TR DEP
Dock
UP SDG

[SW110] [WPH] 1 S·LSW

24A & 26A: to Haslemere, Dorking & Redhill

Platform lengths
1 ⑧
2 ⑧ Up ⑫ Down
3-7 ⑫
8 ⑩

A3
31.20
— 31

UP ASH
DOWN ASH

A
WOKING MINIATURE RAILWAY SOCIETY LTD.
7¼" gauge   1200 metres
Layout still under construction
6/02
N

SANTA'S HALT
TWITCHEN MANOR
BONSEY LANE (alighting platform)
Carriage shed
Station Building
Loco shed
⊠

Miles from Waterloo

Miles from Waterloo via Worplesdon & Guildford (reverse)

WANBOROUGH
34.29
1
2
④
— 32
— 33
— 34
— 35

Aldershot South Jn
50.01

ASH
49.18
49.15 (CCTV-GD)
⑧
1
2
⑤
COM
S·SE S·LSW
2 [GTW] 1
[SW265]
(former Ash Jn)
48.34 | 35.50

[SW265]
[GTW] 1
S·SE

UP BLACKWATER
DN BLACKWATER
UP BCH
DN BRANCH
0.00
[SW123]
NSA S·LSW

24C: to Farnborough
24C: to Aldershot
24C: to Aldershot
24C: to North Camp

A

25B: to Ascot

35

CAMBERLEY 35·30
(CCTV-F) 35·26 (F)
35·37
5:LSW [SW260] AAV
UP FRIMLEY
DN FRIMLEY

Controlled by Feltham (F) ASC

— 37 miles from Waterloo via Twickenham

36

FRIMLEY 37·48
Frimley 31·57
Tunnel
— 38

23: to Woking

BLACKWATER 55·58
GF ④
GTW 2 [SW 265] 5:SE
3708
< M3
Guildford ASC

Controlled from Wokingham (WM)

57 —

56 —

55 —

54 — Miles from Charing Cross via Redhill

UP BLACKWATER 2
DN BLACKWATER 2
54·30 (WM)
(GD)

FARNBOROUGH NORTH 53·16 2
53·11
53·02

Miles from Charing Cross via Redhill

Controlled by Basingstoke (YW) Area Signalling Centre

FARNBOROUGH 33·17 12
3335
GF 'B'

NORTH CAMP 51·18 7
51·22 (CCTV-GD)
A331(t)

Government Sdgs (OOU)
Aldershot (DISC)

ALDERSHOT 35·00 (AS) 34·73
Aldershot GF 'B'

UP MAIN
DOWN MAIN

Miles from Waterloo via Brookwood

31·13 St Catherine's
31·19 (Sand) Tunnel (132 yds)
Shalford Jn 31·42 WPH
5:LSW [SW110]
26A: to Haslemere & Portsmouth
River Wey 41·36-30 41·60
23: to Guildford

B

Tangley (AHB) 39·48
East Shalford 40·20
CHILWORTH 39·15
Chilworth (MCB/CCTV) 39·20

Controlled from Guildford (6D) ASC

Not electrified

Burrows Lane 35·60 (AHB-GD) (GD)(RG)
Brook (AHB) 37·19
36·51 Shere Heath

[SW 300][SW 301] [SO 560]
Gomshall 35·02
GOMSHALL 35·21
35

24B

RSJ S-SE
SHALFORD 41·02
Coombe Lane 32·24

DORKING WEST 30·42
Dorking West 30·50

Not electrified

19A: to Leatherhead
DORKING (DEEPDENE) 29·55
29·65 2·22
Brockham (AHB) 28·08

Controlled by Reigate (RG)

1A: to Reigate & Redhill

BETCHWORTH
Engr's Sdg 27·17 ④
Betchworth 27·21 (CCTV)
26·49
Buckland (AHB)

19A: to Horsham
BTH 3 S-LBSC

29·32-29 River Mole Viaduct

C

RSJ S-SE
[SO560:SW30]

UP READING
DOWN READING
3370-60 Summit
3310 (GD)(RG)

Miles from Charing Cross

HOOK 42·13 10

WINCHFIELD 39·66 11 7
4000
4076

FARNHAM (FN) 40·44
40·33 (CCTV-FN)
40·28
Farnham 40·44

(former Farnham Jn)
COM 39·22 36·75
2 PAA 1 [SW120] 5:LSW

5:LSW BML 1 (London & Southampton)

FLEET 36·38 12

(Bramshott) 35·55

BENTLEY 44·24 6
44·32
Alice Holt 44·11 44·20

Miles from Waterloo via Worplesdon, Guildford (reverse) & Tongham

27B: to Basingstoke

UP SLOW
UP FAST
DOWN FAST
DOWN SLOW

Miles from Waterloo via Worplesdon, Guildford (reverse) & Tongham

EMU Depot
Up Sdgs

Controlled by Basingstoke (YW) Area Signalling Centre

D

24C

45

46

47

48

49 Miles from Waterloo via Worplesdon, Guildford (reverse) & Tongham

50

Controlled by Farnham (FN) SB
Holybourne Oil Sdgs
Star Energy

ALTON 49·13 (339 ft) 8
Mid-Hants NR
former Brewery Sdg 49·39
former Butts Jn 50·19

5:LSW
DOWN ALTON SINGLE UP

MID-HANTS RAILWAY "Watercress Line" (showing altitudes)
(Sep 2000)
MEDSTEAD & FOUR MARKS (644 feet)

Basingstoke
Fareham

ROPLEY (397 feet) 56·52
Dock Sdg
Loca Shed
Z: Pits

Hutchings Sdg
BENNETT'S P SDG 53·46
652'
A1W 5:LSW

Perrins Sdg
ALRESFORD 59·22 (263 feet)
Loading/unloading track

45

46

47

48

49

50

51

52

53

54

55

56

57

58

59

© Copyright Quail Map Company. No reproduction without permission

FELTHAM - READING ● WINDSOR BRANCH ● CHERTSEY BRANCH

A

1A: to Willesden & Waterloo

1A: to Richmond & Waterloo

[SW230] HJW 13.03

Whitton Jn

Hounslow Jn 14.09 14.39

[SW230] HOU S-LSW

Feltham Jn 13.35

S-LSW

[SW210] RDG 1 S-LSW

DOWN MAIN

UP MAIN

Feltham West Grid Sdg GF 'A' (Bedfont La.) 1465 Feltham (CCTV-F) [X](F) ASC 1460

GRID SDG(n) 14.42

FELTHAM 14.68

ASHFORD (Middx) 1740

Staines 19.52
Staines West Jn 19.48

East Yard Emu Berthing Sdgs

Oakmead 18.30

Shortwood Common Crossing 18.44

STAINES 19.02

Staines East Jn 19.26
Staines West Jn

DOWN MAIN UP MAIN

20.40 M25 Bridges

[SW250] SWE S-LSW

SWX

WRAYSBURY 21.40

SUNNYMEADS 22.48

UP WINDSOR
DOWN WINDSOR

Pooley Green (CCTV-MCB) 20.51
EGHAM 21.02

Rusham (AHB) 21.61

Thorpe Lane (CCTV-F) S-LSW

20.60 M25

RDG 1 [SW210] S-LSW

Black Potts Vdct (R. Thames) 24.74 24.63

DATCHET 23.63
Mays (CCTV-F) 23.69

Controlled by Feltham (F) ASC

VIRGINIA WATER 23.15

Stroude 22.51

23.01

24.74
24.65

24.24 24.20

Chertsey 22.32
CHERTSEY 22.25

UP CHERTSEY
DOWN CHERTSEY

23.37 Lyne Bridge (M25) (Rail suspension bridge)

20.65 River Wey 20.71
19.74 Addlestone Jn

ADDLESTONE

(CCTV-F) 22.20

Woking (WK)

[SW255] VWW S-LSW

21B: to Woking

Windsor & Eton RIVERSIDE 25.48

London Road (CCTV-F) 26.66

[SW210] RDG 1 S-LSW

LONGCROSS 25.11

25.40 GF
25.23

SUNNINGDALE 26.71

UP MAIN
DOWN MAIN

-0.02

20.06 River Wey
Reading Spur Jn

[SW255] AJB 21B: to Woking

21B: to Weybridge

[GW03] MLN 1 GW
Reading New Jn
UP RELIEF
UP MAIN
DOWN MAIN
DN R'DG SPUR GW
UP RDG SPUR
UP DN SOUTHERN

To Ealing Broadway and Paddington 3-3A

[RNJ] [SW210]5 R(N)(WM)

Reading Spur Jn
0.80 GW

[SW210] RDG 2 S-SE

Controlled by Reading (R) ASC

27A: Reading

B

25A

ASCOT 28.79

[SW210] RDG 1 S-LSW

Controlled by Feltham (F) ASC

UP MAIN
DOWN MAIN

28.49
28.90

M & EE SDG

NO.5 SDG

29.04

Englemere 29.36

29.18

28.28

DOWN FRIMLEY
UP FRIMLEY

DOWN 30.03 (Ascot West)

UP MAIN
DOWN MAIN

BAGSHOT 32.08

[SW260] AAV S-LSW

Guildford Road Viaduct 32.26 - 32.28

Jenkins Hill 33.23

Bagshot Tunnel (121 yards)

33.60 33.66

24C: to Camberley

24C: to Blackwater

MARTINS HERON 31.09

BRACKNELL 32.24

(WM)(F) 31.20

(F)(P)

A329(M) 34.07

Waterloo LC (AHB) (CCTV-WM)

34.34 34.76

Star Lane (CCTV-WM)

[SW210] RDG 1 S-LSW

Miles from Waterloo via Twickenham

Miles from Waterloo via Weybridge

WOKINGHAM 62.08 62.03

Wokingham LC (WM)

Wokingham Jn COM LC 61.72

35.30
35.73
36.35

Jn

Smiths 35

36.59

WINNERSH 64.10

WINNERSH TRIANGLE 64.72

63.42 M4

UP MAIN
DOWN MAIN

River Loddon 65.16

EARLEY 66.01

Earley 65.70 65.61

66.71

68.35
68.34

2 emu Sdgs
68.48

SANDHURST 57.22

CROWTHORNE 58.66

[SW265] GTW 2 S-SE

UP GUILDFORD
DOWN GUILDFORD

Miles from Charing Cross via Redhill

CHERTSEY BRANCH

This railway track diagram depicts the Portsmouth and Fareham lines. Key locations and features shown include:

Section A (top):
- Chalk Tunnel (845 yds), Controlled by Guildford (GD) ASC
- Shalford Jn 3.42, St Catherine's (Sand) Tunnel (132 yards)
- 23: to Guildford, 24A: to Shalford, Dorking & Redhill
- Farncombe East, Farncombe West, FARNCOMBE 33.40
- R. Wey, GODALMING 34.37
- MILFORD 36.21, WITLEY 38.36
- HASLEMERE 42.79
- LIPHOOK 46.67
- Miles from Waterloo via Woking

Section B (middle):
- ROWLANDS CASTLE 63.18
- Buriton Tunnel (485 yards)
- Idsworth SB, Woodcroft Halt
- LISS 51.35, Liss Common
- Princes Bridge (AHB), Sheet (AHB)
- Kings Fernsden (AHB)
- PETERSFIELD 54.71
- Miles from Waterloo via Woking

Section C (bottom):
- to Botley & Eastleigh, to St Denys & Southampton
- Hamble River Viaduct
- SWANWICK 10.50
- FAREHAM, Fareham Tunnel No.1 (147 yds), Fareham Tunnel No.2 (553 yards)
- Hanson, Newgate Lane (AOCL)
- Bedenham, Wallington Viaduct, Quay Viaduct
- PORTCHESTER 87.35
- COSHAM 90.06, Cosham Jn
- HILSEA 41.41, Portcreek Viaduct, Portcreek Jn
- Farlington Jn, BEDHAMPTON 38.14
- HAVANT 37.40, 20D: to Chichester
- PORTSMOUTH & SOUTHSEA 44.47 (Low Level) Portsmouth, (High Level)
- PORTSMOUTH HARBOUR 45.36, Pier and Arches
- FRATTON 43.64, FRATTON TRAINCARE DEPOT (FR) South West Trains
- Inspection & Carriage Cleaning Shed
- Old Yard, Cattle Dock Sdg, Down Carriage Sdgs
- Blackhars Jn
- Miles from Waterloo via Eastleigh
- Miles from former Southampton Terminus

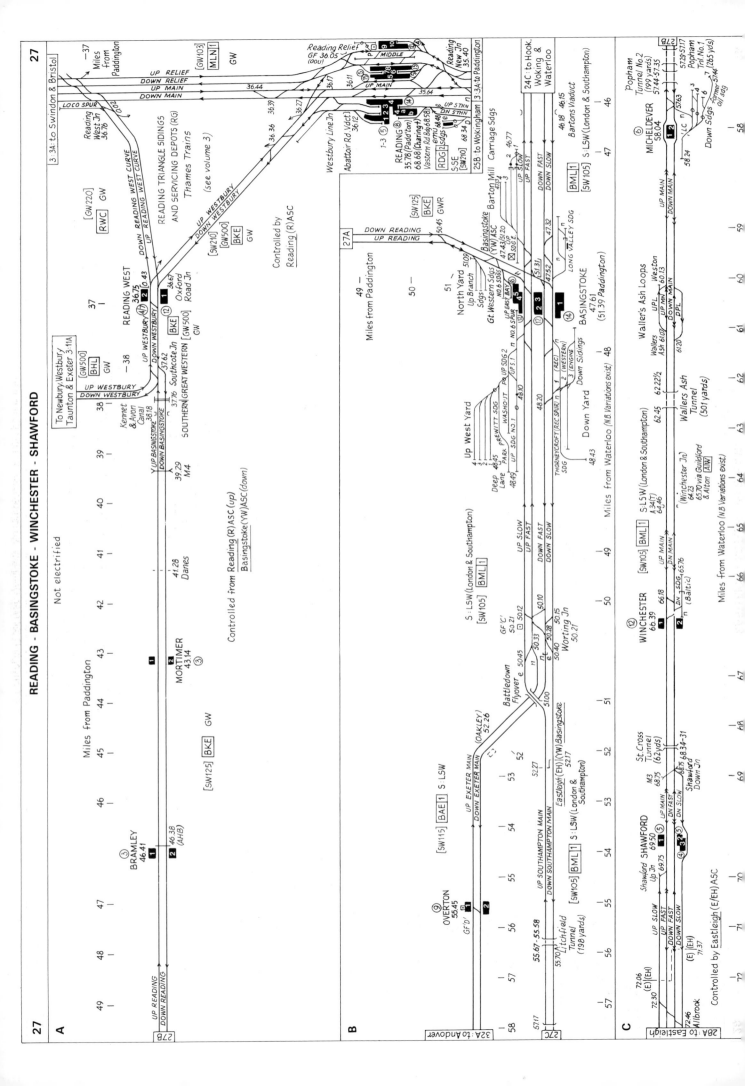

READING - BASINGSTOKE - WINCHESTER - SHAWFORD

27C : to Winchester and Basingstoke

Allbrook 73.10

[SW105] [BML]1 S·LSW (London & Southampton)

UP SLOW
UP FAST
DOWN FAST
DOWN SLOW

72.55
72.46
72.49
72.50
72.52
72.48

EYD 2
EYD 1

Balfour Beatty

Rail Welding Depot

Mowlem Railways

Materials Depot

RECEPTION ROAD NEW
RECEPTION ROAD No.1
RECEPTION ROAD No.2
RECEPTION ROAD No.3

CUTTING NEW
BACK No.1
FRONT
CRANE MIDDLE No.2
BACK No.3

Crane Gantries

Conveyor Lines

Welding Shop

DEPARTURE ROAD

No.15 GDS
PIT SHED ROAD

EASTLEIGH EAST YARD

Dutton Lane
Engineers LC
Engineers Depot

East Yd
GF C

COAL YARD
BACK NECK

GOODS RD1
GOODS RD No.2
E·AST YARD
P·A·D NECK
MAT Transauto
Marcroft Engineering

32C : to Romsey & Salisbury 74.10

[SW130] [ECR] S·LSW

DOWN SALISBURY
UP SALISBURY

Eastleigh East Jn 73.35 / 73.25

Eastleigh (E/EH)ASC 73.17

Eastleigh West Jn 73.48/73.42

EASTLEIGH 73.35

Plat.
1
2
3

UP FAST
DOWN FAST
DOWN SLOW
UP SLOW

73.30 mileage reversal point

Miles from Waterloo

All lines controlled from Eastleigh (E) ASC

SNAKE ROAD
Marcroft Engineering

WB Virtual Quarry
Field Section

FH Young (Transport) Ltd

EASTLEIGH MARSHALLING YARD
Back Roads (12-15)
Former LHS Sdgs (8-11)
Repair Sdgs

[SW105] [BML]1 S·LSW (London & Southampton)

UP MAIN
DOWN MAIN

Steam Shed Sdgs (1-15)
(Stabling Sdgs 1-8)
(Airport Sdgs 9-16)
2-10 electric

F-Fuelling Shed

EASTLEIGH TRACTION & ROLLING STOCK MAINTENANCE DEPOT (EH)
EW&S EYD 7

Former DEMU Shed
Wagon Repair Depot

STABLING ROADS ROAD

Campbell Road 73.60
73.66 / 73.41

DEPOT EXIT ROAD 1
DEPOT EXIT ROAD 2

Eastleigh R.C. (See inset)
EYD 5&6

Campbell Sidings
(1-7, 5 i/se)

Eastleigh South Jn 74.00

PORTSMOUTH SINGLE SIDING
Whitley Stone Terminal

DEMU GF
THROUGH RD
WASHING MACHINE
TANK RD

Eastleigh South Jn
DEPOT ENTRANCE LINE

Chicknal Sdgs
74.06
74.22
74.42
74.45
74.12

Six Arches Bridge
— 75
— 76
HEDGE END 76.76
— 77
— 78

UP PORTSMOUTH
DOWN PORTSMOUTH

[SW135] [ETF] S·LSW

28A

26C : to Fareham

83
82
81
80
79
78

Tapnage Tunnel (122 yds) (Knowle)
81.35-40
81.73
Knowle Viaduct 81.75-78½

KNOWLE SINGLE

Foster Yeoman
DN PORTSM'TH
UP PORTSMOUTH

BOTLEY 78.72
Botley Viaduct 78.43/78.47

[SW135] [ETF] S·LSW

(7) Controlled by Eastleigh (E)ASC

B

EASTLEIGH RENOVATION CENTRE
ALSTOM UK
EYD 5&6

TRAVERSER No.1

INGOING / OUTGOING SDG 73.50

Van Shop
Wheel Store
Sheet Metal
Lift Shop
Bogie Repair
Bays 442-319
Stores
Trimming
Wheel Shop
Mk.3 Area
Paint Shop
Electrical

TRAVERSER No.2

Test Sheds

TRAVERSER No.3

Paint
Repairs
Asbestos
Paint Prime
Shot Blast
Repair

74.16

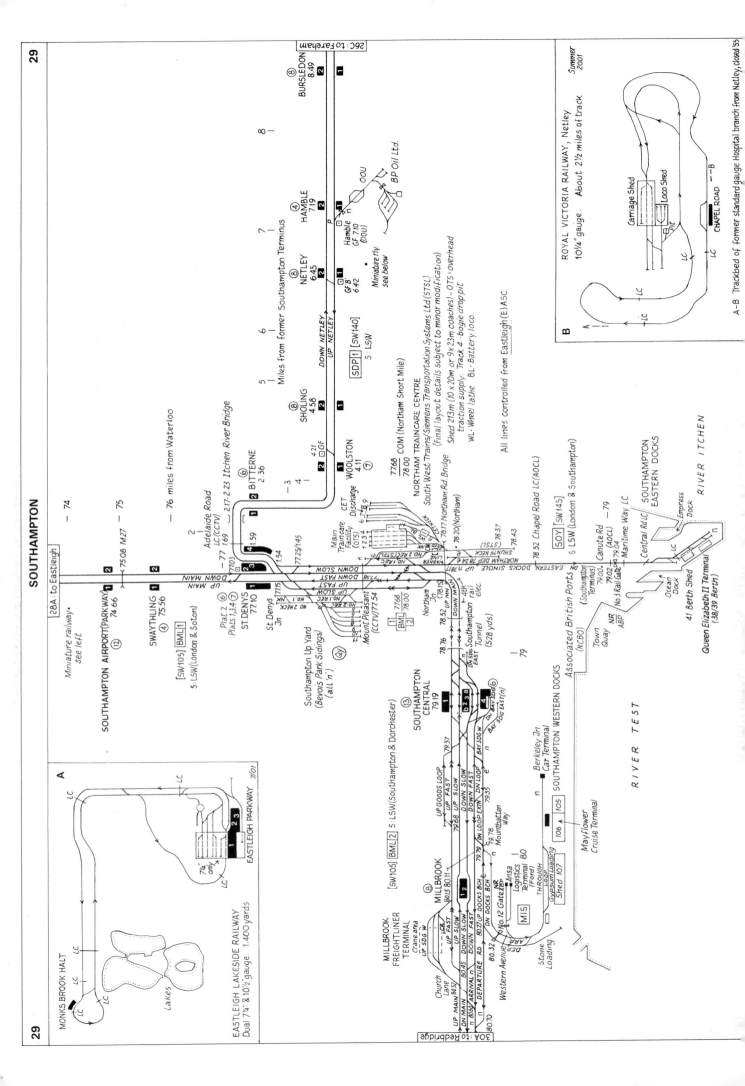

(SOUTHAMPTON) - TOTTON - SWAY ● FAWLEY BRANCH ● LYMINGTON BRANCH

A

Controlled by Brockenhurst (BH)

29: to Southampton

BML2 [SW105]
S: LSW (Southampton & Dorchester)

UP MAIN
DOWN MAIN

Crane area (20 flats)
80.66
Loco Servicing Pnt.
81.42
A
B
LHS
Wagon repair sdgs
Wagon storage sidings

ARRIVAL & DEPARTURE

RTJ1 [SW150] S: LSW
REDBRIDGE
Redbridge Jn ⑦

Depot
GF 'B' Reception Sdgs 81.70
Repair Shop

MARITIME FREIGHTLINER TERMINAL

BML2 [SW105]
S: LSW (Southampton & Dorchester)

32C: to Romsey and Salisbury

UP TEST VALLEY
23J1

R.Test Bridge
23 —

UP MAIN
DOWN MAIN
82.17-15
82.43
82.52
82

* 82.06½ - 82.08
Redbridge Channel Bridge

Totton (Junction) Rd (2)
TOTTON ⑦
Totton (CCTV-E)

High St
ELING TRAMWAY (OOU)

Totton Jn West
83.30
FAWLEY SINGLE
UP
DN
Jacob's Gutter Lane (AHB)
84.12
— 85.11

Curtis 84.11

ASHURST (NEW FOREST)
85.34 ⑥

BML2 [SW105]
S: LSW (Southampton & Dorchester)

BEAULIEU ROAD
88.06 ⑥

Woodfidley
89.59
89.40 (BH)(E)

Miles from Waterloo

Whitley 91.58

UP MAIN
DOWN MAIN

30B

River Test / Marchwood section

88.15
87.45 Crane area
88.00
87.35

Possible Dibden Bay Terminal
Associated British Ports
(distances are estimates)

RIVER TEST
Old Jetty
New Jetty
JETTY HALT

MODEL ROOM HALT
PORT GATE HALT
Regulating Sdgs
South Sdgs
Loading Sidings

MARCHWOOD MILITARY PORT
Sea Mounting Centre : MoD (Army)

Roberts Camp Transport Sdgs (86.75)

Tavell's Lane (AHB) — 86
MULBERRY HALT (MW)
86.06 LC
MARCHWOOD 86.10
Pumpfield Farm R(g) 86.37 Reception & Exchange Sdgs (86.40)
NR (ABP)
Possible Dibden Bay Jn
Veals Lane (AHB)
86.69

Trotts Lane (AHB)
FAWLEY SINGLE
UP DN

HYTHE PIER RAILWAY
2-foot gauge, 240v dc 3rd rail
29 chains
Southampton Water

— 88 West Street (AHB)
88.38
School Road (gates)
88.68
89.31 HYTHE
89 — 90 Hardley GF
91 Hardley (OOU) Inspec
Frost Lane (AHB)
89.60

Fawley Refinery section

Paramins Chlorine Facilities
ZONE 2 (AGW1)
Esso (Anglo Gulf & West Indies)
Loco Shed
Gas Oil
Bitumen
92
91.69
Cadland (E Ave)
CADLANDS
Block 50
LPG Loading
Esso
NR Esso Fawley GF 'C'
91½
91.42
Hardley GF
DISC

FAWLEY 92.10
SWAMP RD (MIDDLE) RD
SHED RD
PLATFM. RD 92.12

FAWLEY REFINERY
TR = Esso/Exxon
Not confirmed by operator

MAIN LINE
Cripple Sdgs
ABB Transportion
TOP SITE
'K' Spur
Crude off loading
Block 9 - Caustic Facilities
Chemical Facilities
Blending

RUNNING ROAD (NIRU)
Chlorine Facilities
Butyl Rubber

Depot 2
CMB

TTF [SW155] 50

B

30A

Lymington Rd (8)
92.55

Luggage Platform GF 92.62
UPL
BROCKENHURST 92.57 (BH)
92.66

BROCKENHURST ⊠

Brockenhurst Jn
UP SDG
UP MAIN
DN MAIN 93.15 93.05
DN/PASS LOOP
DN SDG
SDG

Former 93.60
Lymington Jn
— 94
LYMINGTON SINGLE
UP DN
95.32 (Shirley Holmes)
— 95
— 96
96.61

AMPRESS WORKS (private, closed)
— 97
97.48 Lymington Town ④
LYMINGTON TOWN ④
97.63
97.66 Lymington Viaduct
98.03
Slipway crossing
LYMINGTON PIER ⑧
98.15
9757

BML2 [SW105]
S: LSW

[SW160]
BLP
S: LSW

SWAY ⑦
95.45

Bournem'th 97.08 (WFB)(BH)
Miles from Waterloo
— 98

31A: to Bournemouth
30B

Miles from Waterloo
— 92
92½
— 93

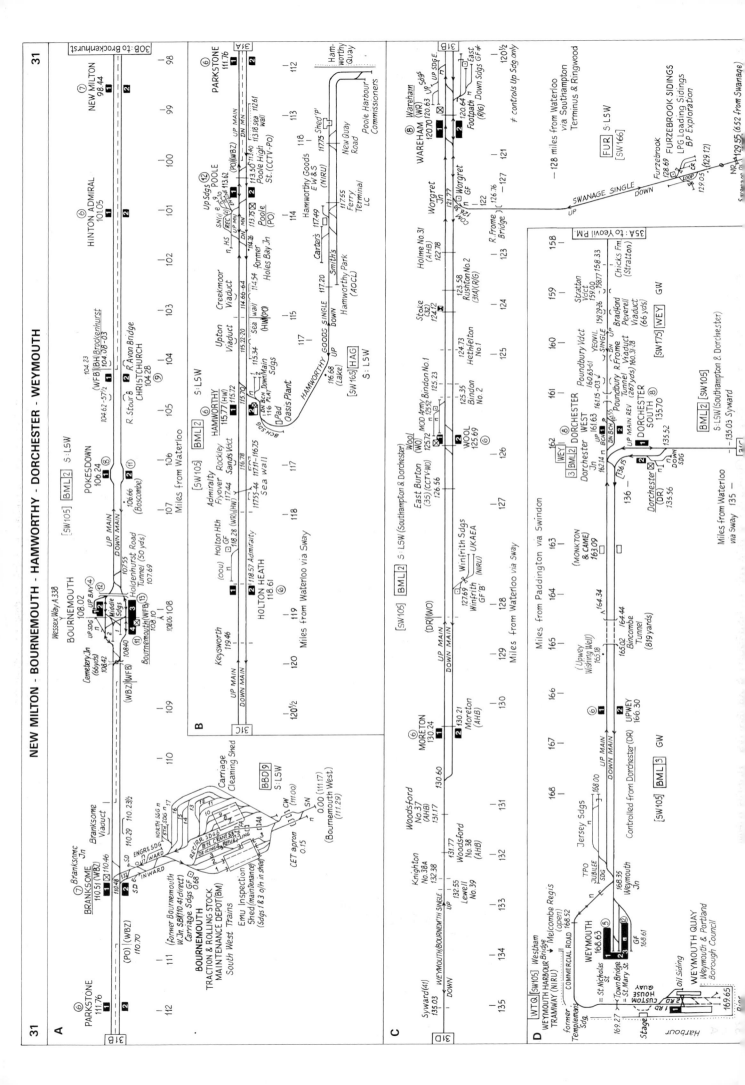

A

27B: to Basingstoke

Not electrified

LUDGERSHALL
Ministry of Defence (Army)
Ludgershall Railhead

Dock 60.8
57.1 5.61
MOD NR
MOD NR
Depot
6.15
Perham
Loading
Dock
Loco Shed
LC Shed
Shed

[SW115] [LUD2] M & S W Jn

(LUDGERSHALL)

— 5
— 4
— 3
— 2
1.71 (Weyhill)
[LUD1]
1.152 A303(T)
0.00
(Red Post Jn)
67.61
Salisbury / Basingstoke

ANDOVER 66.19
Up Yard
EW & S SN
EW & S SN
66.27
66.54 UP BRANCH UP
DOWN SDG
66.48
GFG'
(OOU)
68.42·38(SY)(YW)
A303(T)
GFF'
66.27
[SW115] [BAE]1 S·LSW

WHITCHURCH 59.08
59.36
A34(T)

Phil Hill Brook
or
Monxton
Viaduct

UP EXETER
DOWN EXETER
UP MAIN
DOWN MAIN

Hurstbourne
Viaduct
61.18 - 61.11

62.47

Controlled by Basingstoke (YW) ASC

Miles from Waterloo

GRATELEY 72.49
73.20

58 59 60 61 62 63 64 65 66 67 68 69 70 71 72 73 74

B

33A: to Westbury

Miles from
Paddington
via Swindon

132   (WILTON)
Quidhampton:
Imerys Minerals Ltd
13254
13232

DN WESTBURY
UP WESTBURY
132·33
85·37
Wilton Jn
[SW115] [BAE]2 S·LSW (Salisbury & Yeovil)

Wilton
Sth Jn
86.25
86.18
86.11
A36(T)
UP EXETER
DOWN EXETER
[SW170] GW
13225 Jn GF

UP MAIN
DOWN MAIN
Broadlands Quarry
84.35 H
84·36
A36(T)

Maintenance Shed

SALISBURY
TRAINCARE DEPOT (SA)
South West Trains
CET
DEP SDG 1
DEP 1
8.56.8
CW1
CW2
Ballour
Beatty

[SW115]

Berthing
Sidings
9
8
7
6
5
4
3
2
1
ENGRS
ENGRS
DEPOT·REC
UP MN

Salisbury
East Yard
4
ARR/DEP P
UP MAIN
DN SDG 1 East Carriage
DN SDG 2 Holding Sdgs
(NIRU)
83·28
83.00
82.57
8.255

[2] [BAE]1
COM
84.00 83.72
'Fisherton Short Mile'

PLATFORM
DOWN
1 W BAY
ENGINE
2 3
6
4
83·38 Salisbury (SY)
83.43
Platforms 2 & 3 12
4 14
6 7

Fisherton
Tunnel
A36(T) Tunnel
8263 (443 yds)
SN 8257
82.57

Laverstock
North Jn
82.05
81.78

82.10
82.37
UP
DN MAIN
UP MAIN
DN DEAN
UP DEAN

LAVERSTOCK LOOP
82.39
95·61
Laverstock
South Jn
96·05
96'

Salisbury
Tunnel Jn

(Idmiston)

(Porton)
78.07

Targetts
78.21
77.38

[SW115] [BAE]1 S·LSW

Miles from Waterloo

[LAV] BR (LSW)
[SW115 & 150]

Sir Frederick's Bridge or
Clarendon Park
Viaduct
93.67 92.75

UP MAIN
DOWN MAIN

UP DEAN
DOWN DEAN

East
Grimstead
90.10
P
P
East Grimstead

Controlled from Salisbury (SY)

Miles from Waterloo
via Eastleigh (reverse)

95' 96

Milford
Curve

[SW115] [BAE]1 S·LSW

Bishops
86.73
86.57
Dean Hill
(AHB)
(SY)(E)

[SW150] [RTJ]2 S·LSW
UP DEAN
DOWN DEAN
Controlled from Salisbury (SY)

DEAN 88.10
88.14
(AHB)

Miles from Waterloo via Andover

74 73 72 71 70 69 68 67 66 65 64 63 62 61 60 59 58

74·50·35
[SW150]

C

Not electrified,
except as noted

Crampmoor [SW130] [ECR] S·LSW
78.60
DN SALISBURY SINGLE UP

Halterworth (AHB) 79.24
UP SALISBURY
79.68
DN SALIS
79'
80

(Chandlers
Ford)
75.29
M3
74.46

(Nursling)
M27
21.42
21.51

(Chandlers
Ford)

Mileage from 73.35
Waterloo
reverses at 73.30
74
81.76 Redbridge Jn

Eastleigh
(E/EH) ASC
73.17
73.25

28A: to
Basingstoke
[BML]1

28A: Eastleigh
e
e
e
30A: to Southampton
23.37
23.31

23.02 23.13
Chandlers
22.32
Banks
30A: to Totton
[BML]2

Romsey (T)
UP SDG GF 80.50·35
ROMSEY 80.47
81.16 (SY)(E)
Test River
Bridge
(20)
81.18

[2][6]
[SW150] [RTJ]1 S·LSW

Controlled from Eastleigh (E) ASC
UP TEST VALLEY
DOWN TEST VALLEY
Miles from Andover Jn via Stockbridge

DUNBRIDGE
Dunbridge 84.37
84.24
(AHB·X)

Butler's
83.05
83.45
Kimbridge
(AHB·X)

82.60
82.30
Thurstons Terrys

Miles from Waterloo via Eastleigh (reverse)

89 88 87 86 85 84 83 82 81 80 79 78 77 76 75 74 73 22 21 20 19 23

32B

© Copyright Quail Map Company. No reproduction without permission

32

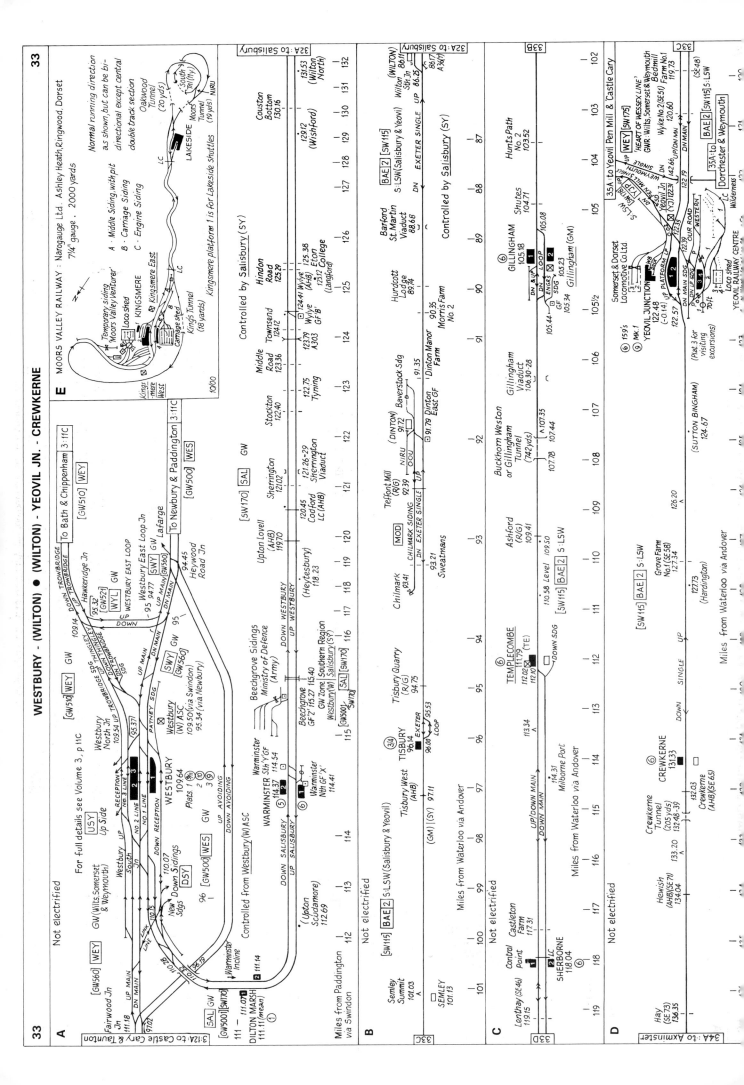

CHARD JUNCTION - EXETER & EXMOUTH BRANCH • SEATON TRAMWAY • BICTON WOODLAND RAILWAY

A

Not electrified

33D: to Yeovil Jn

Honiton Tunnel (1345 yds)
153½
153.26
152.45

151.47
(Honiton Incline Box)

Black Sand Bridge A35(r)
150.13

Miles from Waterloo via Andover

Marshwood Farm No.2 (SE76)
138.78

Chard Junction (CJ)
139.35 ⊠ 139.24
139.32
MAIN
LOOP (SE77) 'St./vel'
Chard Jn 3 (00U)
Down Sdgs GF
139.48

Westford Foot (SE78)
139.65
13964

← DOWN

34A

Honiton GF (HN)
154.62 154.60
PW ⊠ LOOP
154.76 154.44
MAIN
HONITON 154.56 ⑥

(Roundball)
155.23

B EXMOUTH JUNCTION

West Sdgs 5 4 3 2 1
Workshop
LONG VALLEY
Plant Depot
Amey Rail : Jarvis
SIDING   DOWN WATERLOO
ARR   UP WATERLOO
FUEL GANTRY RD
LC (barriers)
170.27
POLSLOE BRIDGE 0.34 ⑥ ⊠
EW & S
170.44
-0.01 ⊠ Exmouth Jn (EJ)
170.21 0.00
UP   EXMOUTH
DOWN

PINHOE 168.44 ❶
168.39
Pinhoe (CCTV-EJ) ❷
168.24 168.09 1674J
M5 167J-4½%

Oxenlears (SE92)
145.78

Abbey Farm No.2 (SE90)
145.15 145.20
Slylakes (SE91)
145.46

Axminster (SE84/CCTV)
144.15
Control Point 'A'
144.41
AXMINSTER 144.41 ⑥

Broom (AHB) (SE79)
14.14
Axe (AHB)
141.56

BAE 2 SW115   S:LSW

← DOWN

(SEATON JUNCTION)
147.63

(Broadclyst)
166.57
167.12

'GATEWAY' Railfreight Terminal

Proposed (c.35 chains)

Cranmaford (SE111)(AHB)
165.20
164.30 GT. WESTERN / SOUTHERN REGION ZONE
SW115

WHIMPLE 163.02 ③

Controlled from Exmouth Jn (EJ)

Not electrified

Controlled from Honiton (HN)

BAE 2 SW115   S:LSW

FENITON 159.24
Feniton (SE02)159.27 ③ (F)

River Otter Viaduct (79 yards)
158.28 157.9-75
A30(r)

Miles from Waterloo via Andover

C

GW108 MLN 1
GW (South Devon)
To Newton Abbot & Plymouth
3:7B

UP MN 194.17
DOWN MAIN

Exeter (E)/ASC
194.00
R. Exe
194.09-07
Exeter St Davids Jn
172.04
EXETER ST. DAVIDS
194.00
172.04
Platforms 1 ①②
③④ ⑦⑫
⑤⑥⑭

Red Cow (CCTV-E)
193.62
Westyard
UP PASSENGER LP
DOWN MAIN UM
UP MAIN
DOWN RELIEF
UP RELIEF
6a 5 6
3a 4 3
1a 1 2
Hyde Park Sdg

Riverside Yard: EW&S
193.37
UP GOODS RECEPTION
DOWN GOODS DEPARTURE
UP MAIN
DOWN MAIN
193.49
193.72 SHUNT SPUR
WATERLOO YD
New Yard
193.27 Cowley Bridge Jn

GW   MLN 1 GW108

193 Miles from Paddington via Box
of 18c S:LSW mileage adjustment
To Barnstaple
DAC GW606 S:LSW
To Taunton, Bristol & Paddington
(Padn)192.52

UP GDS (W)1100 lb
UP 50 GDS
UP GDS

GREAT WESTERN ZONE

For full details see Volume 3, page 7A

Exeter Central Goods Jn
171.30
EXETER CENTRAL
171.30

St Davids Tunnel (184 yards)
SD

171.61
171.53
UP WLOO
DOWN WLOO
TRAP
171.43
3 ⑬

Exeter Central Goods Jn
171.30
171.07
St. James Park ②
170.72
Miles from Waterloo via Andover
170.56
Blackboy Tunnel (262 yards)
170.44

DN/UP WATERLOO
UP WATERLOO
SW115 GW610
BAE 2
17153
S:LSW
DN BAY
B ⑬ ❶
DN

D SEATON & DISTRICT ELECTRIC TRAMWAY

2' 9" gauge. 120v DC overhead. 2¾ miles

SEATON (441)
Windy Corner
Riverside Depot
Poppy Corner
Leeds Bridge Riverside
4.01
RIVER AXE
S:LSW
Axmouth Loop
3.47
Bobsworth Bridge
3.22
Swan's Nest Loop
3.15
Colyford
2.57
River Coly (A3052)
2.54
Tye Lane Loop
2.38
Cownhayne Loop
2.01
Cownhayne Request Stop 1.61
COLYTON

LC (AOCL)
2 miles from Seaton Jn
10/00

E BICTON WOODLAND RAILWAY (BWR)

1' 6" gauge. 1896 yards

Works
BICTON ②
The Lake
Hermitage Drive (open)
Pine Jn 54
23
Roundball
LAKESIDE (NIRU)
LC (foot) 62
LC (foot) 64
59
16
18
19
LC (foot)
LC
73
76 78
THE HERMITAGE

6/02

© Copyright Quail Map Company. No reproduction without permission

❶ DIGBY & SOWTON 2.20
C(2.46)(A379)
M5
TOPSHAM 4.26 ❷❶
4.23 Topsham (CCTV-EJ)
4.20
4.38
4.79
5.04
River Clyst Viaduct (114 yards)
5.39 Water Lane
EXTON ⑤ 5.67
557 Daws Lane
LYMPSTONE COMMANDO 6.23 ⑤

Branch controlled from Exmouth Junction (EJ)

LYMPSTONE VILLAGE 7.28
sea wall
7.73
8.18²
sea wall 8.36½
8.68¾
EXMOUTH 9.32 ❶ ⑤

34B
34C
34

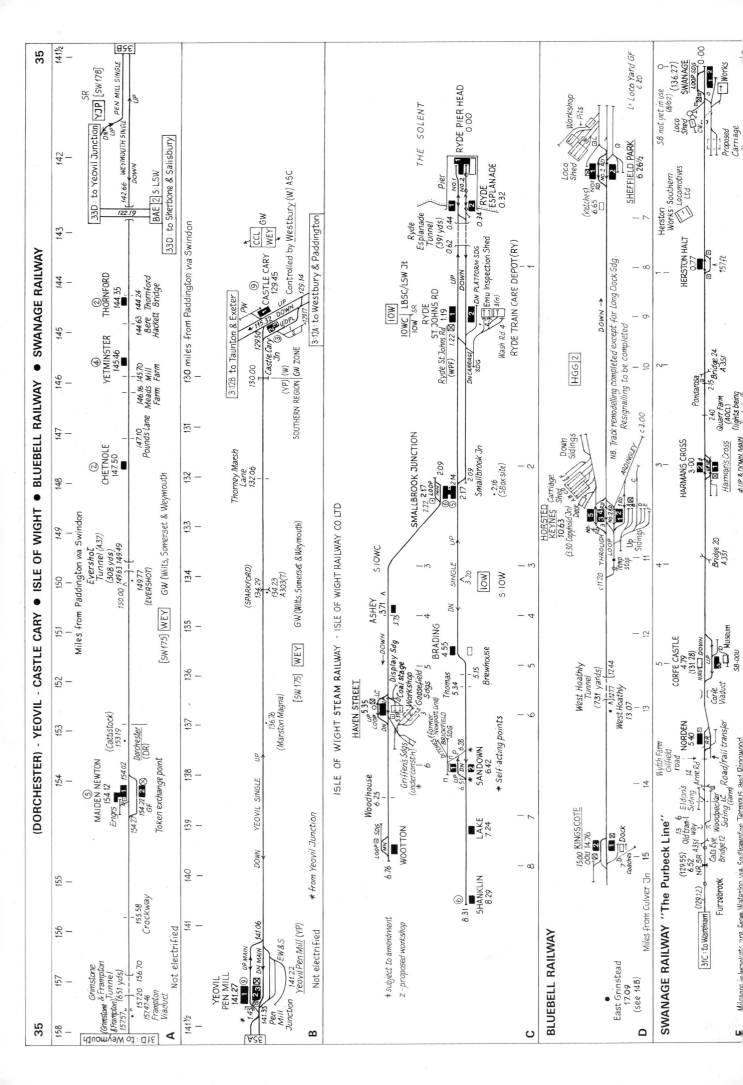

(DORCHESTER) - YEOVIL - CASTLE CARY ● ISLE OF WIGHT ● BLUEBELL RAILWAY ● SWANAGE RAILWAY

BLUEBELL RAILWAY

ISLE OF WIGHT STEAM RAILWAY - ISLE OF WIGHT RAILWAY CO LTD

SWANAGE RAILWAY "The Purbeck Line"

VARIOUS MINOR RAILWAYS

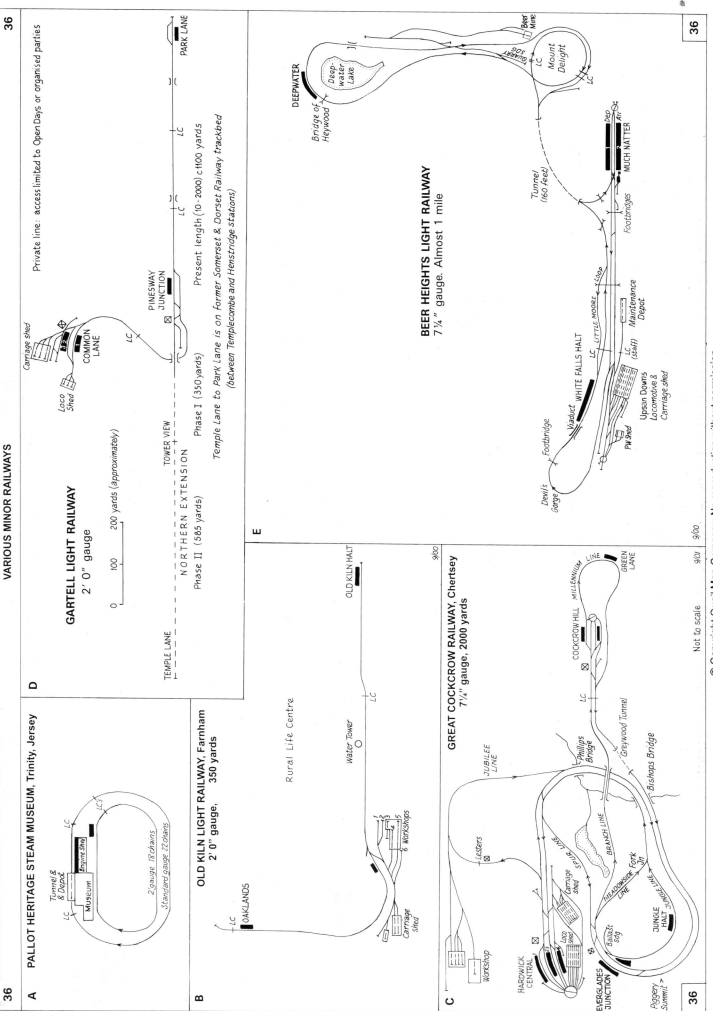

A PALLOT HERITAGE STEAM MUSEUM, Trinity, Jersey

D GARTELL LIGHT RAILWAY

2' 0" gauge

Private line: access limited to Open Days or organised parties

0   100   200 yards (approximately)

NORTHERN EXTENSION
Phase I (350 yards)
Phase II (585 yards)

Present length (10–2000) c1100 yards

Temple Lane to Park Lane is on former Somerset & Dorset Railway trackbed
(between Templecombe and Henstridge stations)

TEMPLE LANE
TOWER VIEW
PINESWAY JUNCTION
COMMON LANE
Loco Shed
Carriage shed
PARK LANE
LC

2' gauge 18 chains
Standard gauge 22 chains
Tunnel & Depot
Engine Shed
Museum
LC
LC3

B OLD KILN LIGHT RAILWAY, Farnham
2' 0" gauge, 350 yards

Rural Life Centre
Water Tower
OLD KILN HALT
LC
OAKLANDS
Carriage Shed
Workshops
1 2 3 4 5 6

E

C GREAT COCKCROW RAILWAY, Chertsey
7¼" gauge, 2000 yards

JUBILEE LINE
COCKCROW HILL
MILLENNIUM LINE
GREEN LANE
Greywood Tunnel
Bishops Bridge
Phillips Bridge
SPUR LINE
BRANCH LINE
MEADOWSIDE FORK Jn
JUNGLE LINE
JUNGLE HALT
Lesters
Ballast Sdg
Carriage shed
Loco Shed
Workshop
HARDWICK CENTRAL
EVERGLADES JUNCTION
Piggery Summit
LC
9/00

Not to scale   9/01

BEER HEIGHTS LIGHT RAILWAY
7¼" gauge. Almost 1 mile

DEEPWATER
Bridge of Heywood
Deep-water Lake
Beer Mine
QUARRY SDG
Mount Delight
LC
LC
Tunnel (160 feet)
Dep Arr
1 2
MUCH NATTER
LOOP
LITTLE MOORE
LC (staff)
Maintenance Depot
WHITE FALLS HALT
Viaduct
Upsan Downs Locomotive & Carriage shed
Pw Shed
Footbridges
Footbridge
Devil's Gorge
9/00   9/01

© Copyright Quail Map Company. No reproduction without permission

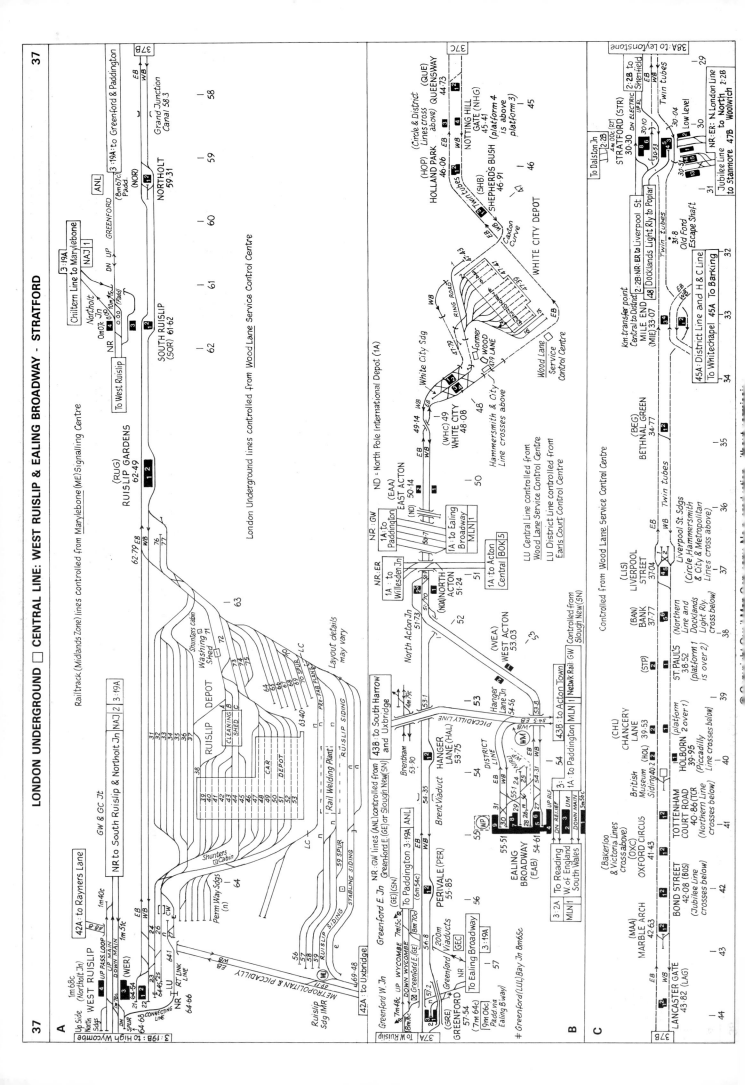

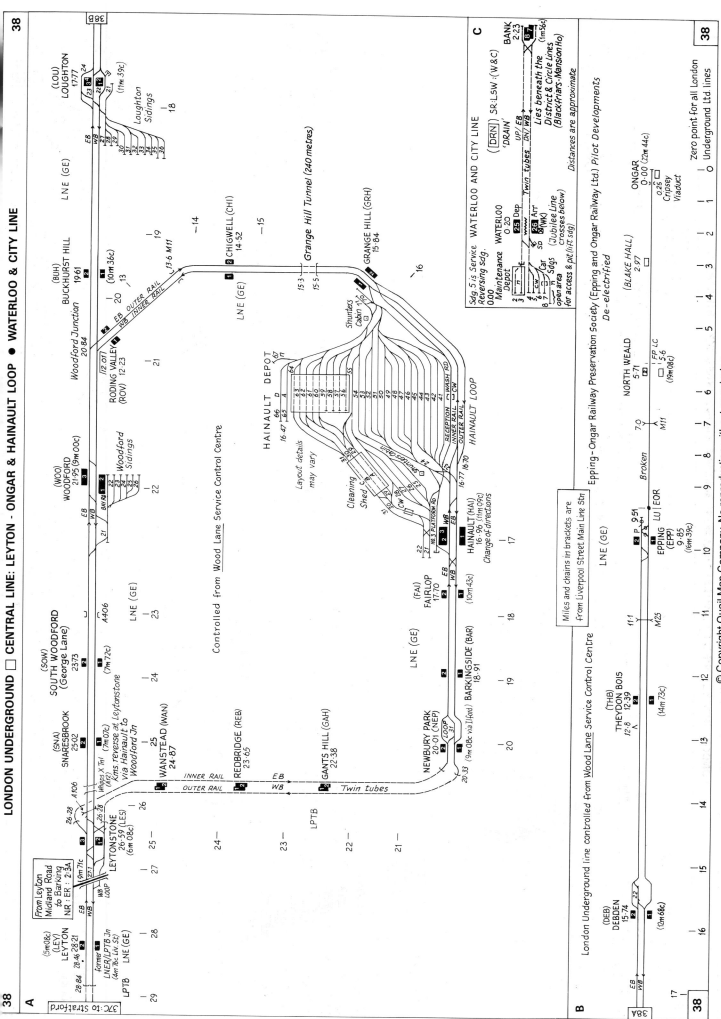

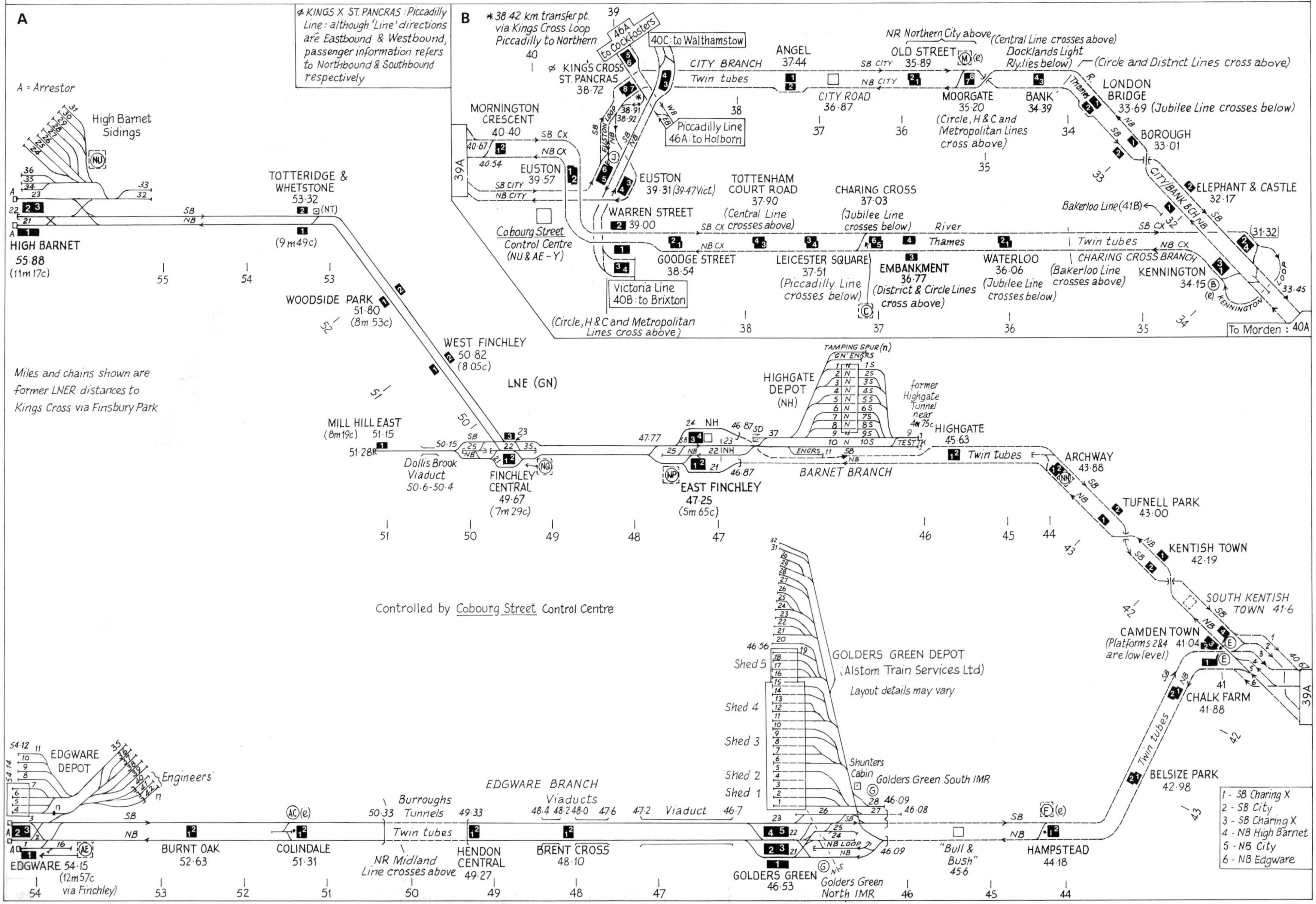
A
A = Arrestor
High Barnet Sidings
HIGH BARNET
55·88
(11m 17c)
TOTTERIDGE & WHETSTONE
53·32
(9m49c)
WOODSIDE PARK
51·80
(8m 53c)
WEST FINCHLEY
50·82
(8 05c)
LNE (GN)
MILL HILL EAST
(8m19c) 51·15
Dollis Brook Viaduct
50·6-50·4
FINCHLEY CENTRAL
49·67
(7m 29c)
EAST FINCHLEY
47·25
(5m 65c)
HIGHGATE DEPOT
(NH)
TAMPING SPUR (n)
former Highgate Tunnel
HIGHGATE
45·63
Twin tubes
BARNET BRANCH
ARCHWAY
43·88
TUFNELL PARK
43·00
KENTISH TOWN
42·19
SOUTH KENTISH TOWN 41·6
CAMDEN TOWN
(Platforms 2&4 are low level) 41·04
CHALK FARM
41·88
BELSIZE PARK
42·98
HAMPSTEAD
44·18
"Bull & Bush"
45·6
GOLDERS GREEN DEPOT
(Alstom Train Services Ltd)
Layout details may vary
Shed 5
Shed 4
Shed 3
Shed 2
Shed 1
Shunters Cabin
Golders Green South IMR
Golders Green North IMR
GOLDERS GREEN
46·53
EDGWARE BRANCH
Viaducts
Viaduct
BRENT CROSS
48·10
HENDON CENTRAL
49·27
Burroughs Tunnels
NR Midland Line crosses above
COLINDALE
51·31
BURNT OAK
52·63
EDGWARE DEPOT
Engineers
EDGWARE 54·15
(12m 57c via Finchley)
Miles and chains shown are former LNER distances to Kings Cross via Finsbury Park
Controlled by Cobourg Street Control Centre
1 - SB Charing X
2 - SB City
3 - SB Charing X
4 - NB High Barnet
5 - NB City
6 - NB Edgware
B
ϕ KINGS X ST. PANCRAS : Piccadilly Line : although 'Line' directions are Eastbound & Westbound, passenger information refers to Northbound & Southbound respectively
* 38·42 km transfer pt. via Kings Cross Loop Piccadilly to Northern
46A to Cockfosters
40C: to Walthamstow
Piccadilly Line 46A: to Holborn
Victoria Line 40B: to Brixton
MORNINGTON CRESCENT
40·40
EUSTON
39·57
KING'S CROSS ST. PANCRAS
38·72
EUSTON
39·31 (39·47 Vict.)
WARREN STREET
39·00
GOODGE STREET
38·54
Cobourg Street Control Centre
(NU & AE - Y)
(Circle, H & C and Metropolitan Lines cross above)
CITY BRANCH
Twin tubes
ANGEL
37·44
CITY ROAD
36·87
NR Northern City above
OLD STREET
35·89
MOORGATE
35·20
(Circle, H & C and Metropolitan Lines cross above)
(Central Line crosses above)
Docklands Light Rly. lies below)
(Circle and District Lines cross above)
BANK
34·39
LONDON BRIDGE
33·69 (Jubilee Line crosses below)
BOROUGH
33·01
ELEPHANT & CASTLE
32·17
CITY/BANK BCH
TOTTENHAM COURT ROAD
37·90
(Central Line crosses above)
LEICESTER SQUARE
37·51
(Piccadilly Line crosses below)
CHARING CROSS
37·03
(Jubilee Line crosses below)
EMBANKMENT
36·77
(District & Circle Lines cross above)
River Thames
WATERLOO
36·06
(Jubilee Line crosses below)
Twin tubes
CHARING CROSS BRANCH
(Bakerloo Line crosses above)
Bakerloo Line (41B)
KENNINGTON
34·15
KENNINGTON LOOP
To Morden : 40A
39A

LONDON UNDERGROUND ☐ NORTHERN LINE: OVAL - MORDEN ● VICTORIA LINE

A

MORDEN DEPOT

(Alstom Train Services Ltd)

1 2 3 4 5 6 7 8 9 10 11 12 13 14 15 16 17
18 19 20 21 22 23 24 25
26 27 28 29 30 31 32

21·32 27(n) 21·36 21·39 21·39

Paint Shop

Controlled by Cobourg Street Control Centre, except '27'(Morden Depot)

SD 21·93 CW 54
41 44 45 SD 21·89 CW 55
22·31 1 2 3 42 4 5 43 Y Z
MORDEN 22·15

STOCKWELL 31·91
40B : to Brixton
Victoria Line
40B : to Walthamstow
47·13 Victoria Line

CLAPHAM NORTH 31·09

CLAPHAM COMMON 30·47

CLAPHAM SOUTH 29·21

BALHAM 28·06

TOOTING BEC 27·08

TOOTING BROADWAY 25·97

COLLIERS WOOD 24·75

SOUTH WIMBLEDON (MERTON) 23·61

Twin tubes

OVAL 33·26
33·20

39B : to Kennington

B

40 (Charing Cross branch of Northern Line crosses 1 above)

41B : to Baker St Bakerloo Line
WARREN STREET 40·22
40C
(Circle, Met. and H & C Lines cross above)

OXFORD CIRCUS 41·14
(Central Line crosses below)

41B : to Elephant

GREEN PARK 42·23
(Jubilee and Piccadilly Lines cross below)

VICTORIA 43·35
(District & Circle Lines cross above)
Victoria Sidings

PIMLICO 44·57

VAUXHALL 45·37
River Thames

STOCKWELL 47·13

40A : to Kennington Northern Line

40A : to Morden

BRIXTON 48·61
49·02 22 Pit

Controlled by Cobourg Street Control Centre

Twin tubes

C

Staff Platforms
18 Wheel Lathe Shed 19 20
21 22 23 24 25S 25N 26S 26N 27S 27N 28S 28N 29S 29N 30S 30N 31S 31N 32S 32N 33S 33N 34S 34N 35S 35N

Car Sheds 25-35 Stabling Sdgs
36-38 Workshops
39-41 Inspection/Cleaning

28·56
28·79
28·84

NORTHUMBERLAND PARK DEPOT

NR–Lea Valley Line UP DOWN

37 38 39 40 41 42 43 44 45 46 47 48 54 55 56 57

29·08
36

Layout details may vary

Depot Control Tower (NP)
29 CW
Staff Platform
Staff Platform 27

Northumberland Park Depot IMR 29·45
Northumberland 29·71 30

WALTHAMSTOW CENTRAL 27·33
22 26·98
21

BLACKHORSE ROAD 28·79
Twin tubes

TOTTENHAM HALE 30·15

SEVEN SISTERS 31·19
62 63

FINSBURY PARK 34·34
46A : to Earls Court
Piccadilly Line 46A/B : to Cockfosters
34·51
Twin tubes
km transferpoint Piccadilly to Victoria

HIGHBURY & ISLINGTON 36·29

2 : 14A (Northern City Line) NR
To Moorgate   To Finsbury Park
(2m 21c Moorgate)

KINGS CROSS ST PANCRAS 38·72
(Northern and Piccadilly Lines cross below)

46A : to Piccadilly Line

EUSTON 39·47
(Northern Line [Charing + Bch] crosses above)

WARREN STREET 40·22

39B : To Camden Town : Northern Line : to Bank (City Branch)

40B

(Circle, Met, H & C Lines cross above)

 # these are line directions, passenger information refers to Northbound (↑) & Southbound (↓)

Controlled by Cobourg Street Control Centre, except 'NP' (Northumberland Park Depot)

© Copyright Quail Map Company. No reproduction without permission

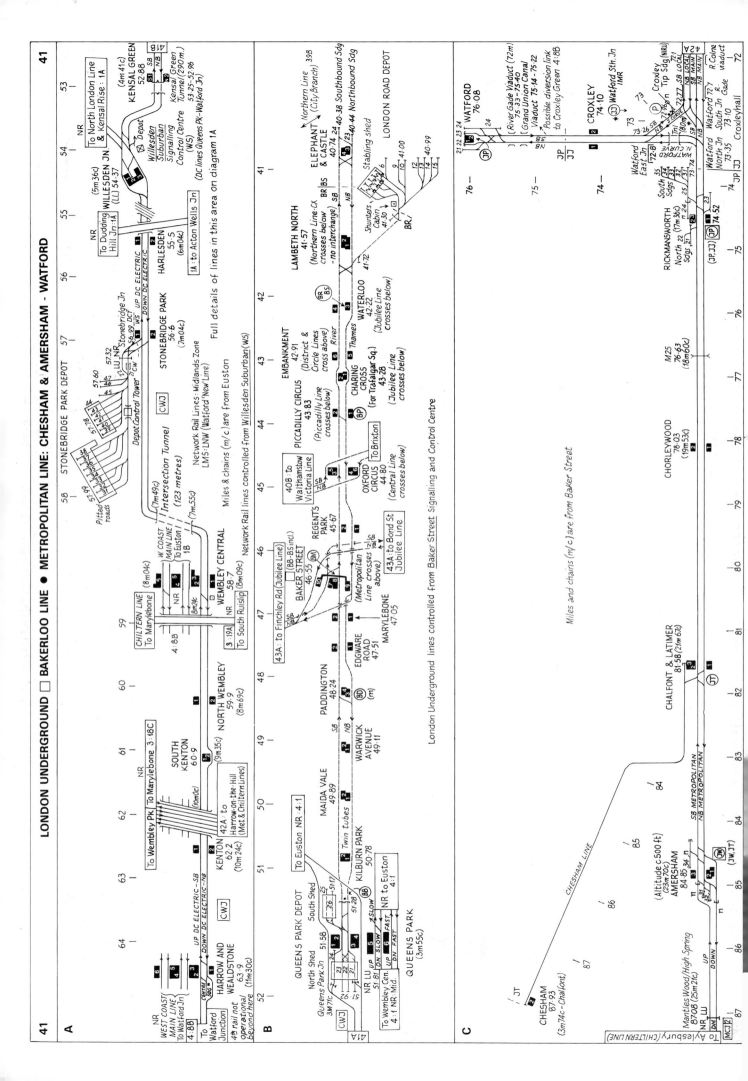

42   42

LONDON UNDERGROUND □ METROPOLITAN LINE: MOOR PARK & UXBRIDGE - (FINCHLEY ROAD) ● JUBILEE LINE: STANMORE - WEST HAMPSTEAD

A

Jubilee Line controlled from Baker Street: Metropolitan & Jubilee Signalling Control Centre

42B

PRESTON ROAD 58·84
59

KINGSBURY 60·23
60

To Harrow & W.
NORTHWICK PARK 60·49

SB FAST
SB LOCAL
NB LOCAL 59
NB FAST
UP HARROW
DOWN HARROW

70m00c (Euston)
NR
To Euston 4·8B
41A: to Queens Park Bakerloo Line

QUEENSBURY 61·56
61

CANONS PARK 63·27
JUBILEE LINE
63

HARROW-ON-THE-HILL 61·78
SB LOCAL 61·78

Subsidiary
(JB) South 61
62

LU NR 61·25 (197m05ch Manchester London Rd.
9m13ch Baker St.)
Harrow South Jn 61·56
(JB) North

WEST HARROW 63·03
63

Harrow North Jn
62·83

NB UXBRIDGE
SB UXBRIDGE

Rayners Lane Jn 64·33 (km. transfer point Piccadilly to Metropolitan)
43B: to Acton Town (Piccadilly Line)

Stanmore Sidings

STANMORE 64·62
SB
NB
SD
33
T = Tamping Machine Spur (n)

32 31 30 29 28 27 26 25 24 23
22 T 21

PINNER 65·25
65

NORTH HARROW 63·77
64

RAYNERS LANE 64·41
(MP, MU, MW)
65

EASTCOTE 66·14
EB
WB
66

RUISLIP MANOR 67·28
67

NORTHWOOD HILLS 67·33

NORTHWOOD 68·95
69
22(n) PW
21

37A: to W. Ruislip
LU Central
NR Chiltern Line
To Ruislip Depot 37A: to S. Ruislip

RUISLIP 68·00
68

A = spur road/rail vehicle transfer point

ICKENHAM 69·85
70

RUISLIP SDGS 69·48 69
n5ch

MOOR PARK 71·16
(15m 28c - Baker St.)
71

41C: to Watford & Amersham

METROPOLITAN & PICCADILLY LINES

HILLINGDON (Swakeleys) 70·93
71

SB LOCAL
NB LOCAL
SB MAIN
NB MAIN
72

72·30 Uxbridge Jn
72

Uxbridge Sidings

38 37 36 35 34 33 32 31 30 29 28 27 26 25 24 23
EB
WB

UXBRIDGE 73·03
(MW)
21

B

Jubilee Line controlled from Baker Street: Metropolitan & Jubilee Signalling Control Centre

LONDON UNDERGROUND DISTANCES
(From June 1972)

Distances are measured in kilometres from an origin 0.000 at the former terminus at Ongar. Distances, denoted with posts/plates every 0.2 km, proceed westwards along the Central line to its termini at West Ruislip and Ealing Broadway.

Distances on other lines are calculated via the following 'transfer locations' from which measurements may increase or decrease.

From Line	To Line	Transfer Point	Distance
Central	District	Mile End	33·1
District	East London	St. Mary's Jn	33·45
District	Piccadilly	Barons Court	47·8
Piccadilly	Metropolitan	Rayners Lane	64·4
Piccadilly	Victoria	Finsbury Park	34·5
Piccadilly	Northern	Kings Cross Loop	38·4
Metropolitan	Jubilee	Finchley Road	50·1
Jubilee	Bakerloo	Baker Street	46·5

LU lines controlled from Baker Street: Met. & Jubilee Signalling Control Centre
NR lines controlled from Marylebone Area Signalling Centre

43A: to Finchley
NR : ER
To Gospel Oak: 2·1A
WEST HAMPSTEAD 50·75
51·3
MD/JD
51

North London Line to Willesden Jn

To Cricklewood
NR : ER
DOLLIS HILL 54·24
54·8
201m09c
54

KILBURN 51·84
203m2lc
52

WILLESDEN GREEN 53·03
(JE) 53·03
METROPOLITAN SB
JUBILEE SB
JUBILEE NB
METROPOLITAN NB
UP MAIN
DOWN MAIN
53

To Neasden & Acton Wells Jns
1A

NEASDEN 55·09
55·07
5
200m66c
Neasden Sbth Jn
Neasden Jn
56

Neasden Freight Terminal - See 3/18C
1A: to South Ruislip

NEASDEN DEPOT
Layout details may vary

South End

Neasden Service Control Centre for Jubilee Line Extension only (Green Park) to Stratford
(2M NM)

Chemical Washing Shed
CAR DEPOT
Klondyke Sidings

Neasden Depot Train Movements Room

North End

Permanent Way Sdgs
108 n

MCJ1

NR: Midlands Zone CHILTERN LINE

WEMBLEY PARK 57·38
(MG)
6
57·09
DEPOT RD SB
DEPOT RD NB
57

Wembley Park Sidings 36 35 34 33 32
31·30a

MET SB FAST
MET SB LOCAL
JUB SB LOCAL
JUB SB
JUBILEE NB
MET NB LOCAL
MET NB FAST
UP HARROW
DOWN HARROW
58

SB 8·2
(JG)
42B

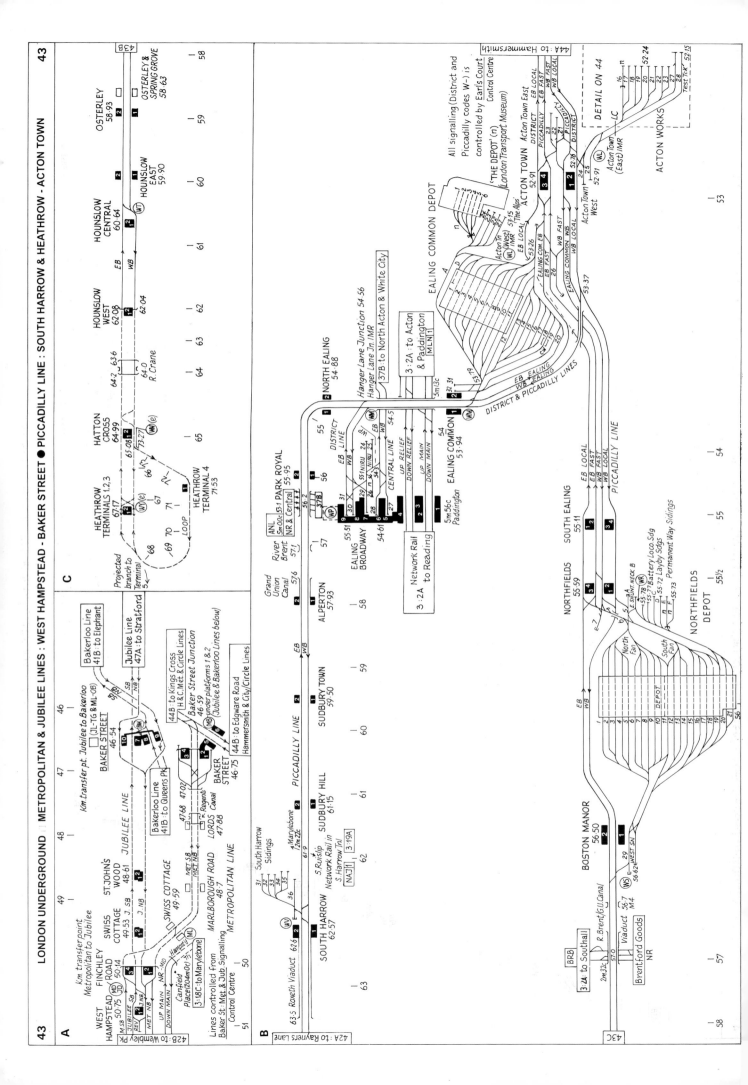

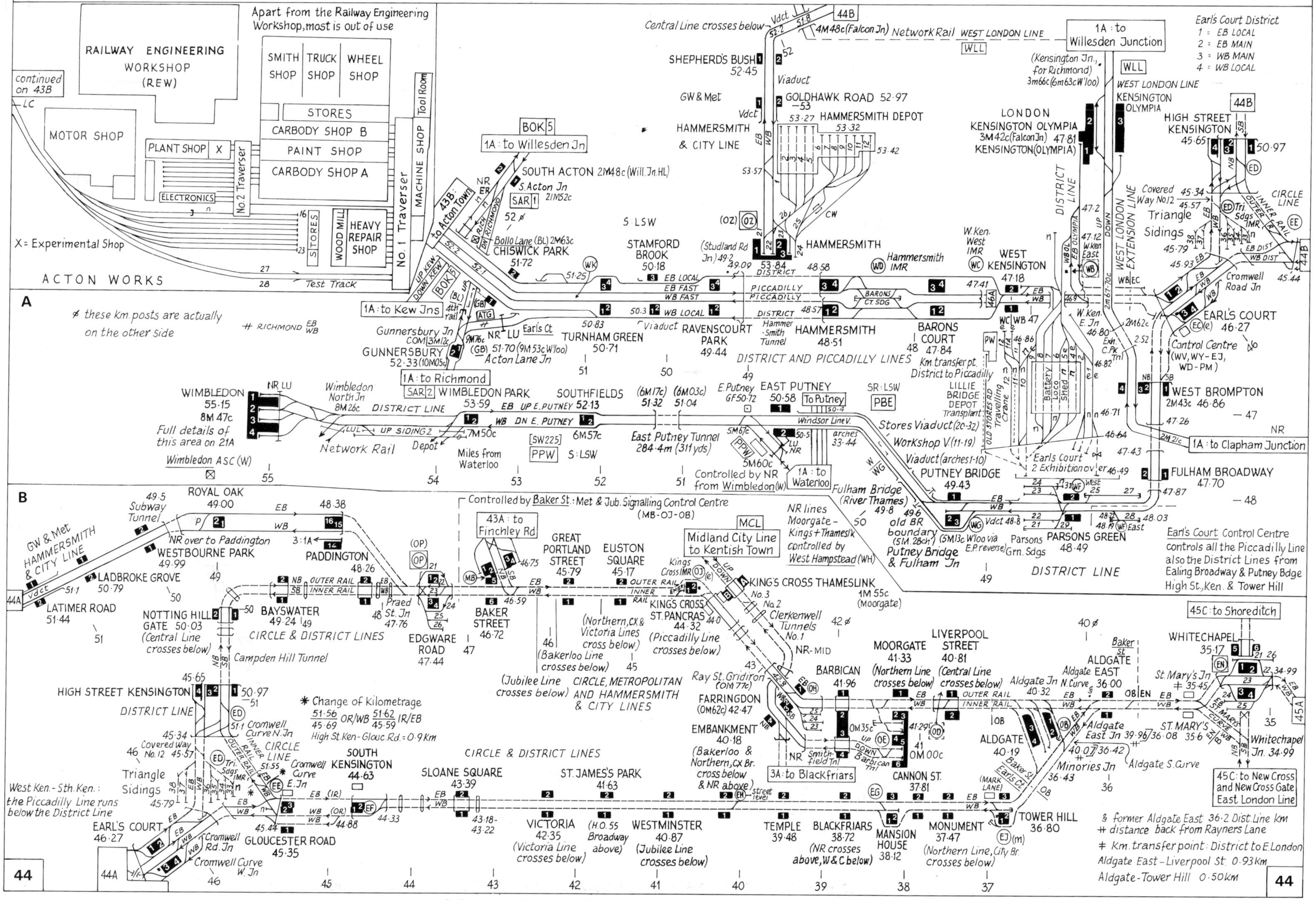

LONDON UNDERGROUND ☐ DISTRICT, PICCADILLY, METROPOLITAN, HAMMERSMITH & CITY LINES: CENTRAL AREA ● CIRCLE LINE

© Copyright Quail Map Company. No reproduction without permission

(Technical railway track schematic diagram. Principal labels transcribed below.)

Stations and locations:

HIGH STREET KENSINGTON 45 65 · 45 34
KENSINGTON OLYMPIA
LONDON KENSINGTON OLYMPIA
EARLS COURT 46 27
WEST BROMPTON 2M43c 46 86 — 47
FULHAM BROADWAY 47 70
BARONS COURT 48 · 47 84
HAMMERSMITH 48 51 · 48 57
SHEPHERDS BUSH 52 45
GOLDHAWK ROAD 52 97 — 53
HAMMERSMITH DEPOT 53 32 · 53 42
HAMMERSMITH & CITY LINE
STAMFORD BROOK 50 18
RAVENSCOURT PARK 49 44
TURNHAM GREEN 50 71
CHISWICK PARK 51 72
SOUTH ACTON 2M48c (Will Jn HL)
SOUTHFIELDS 52 13
EAST PUTNEY 50-58
PUTNEY BRIDGE 49 43
PARSONS GREEN 48 49
WIMBLEDON PARK
WIMBLEDON 55 15 · 8M 47c
GUNNERSBURY
RAILWAY ENGINEERING WORKSHOP (REW)
ACTON WORKS

Right / lower section:

WHITECHAPEL 35 17 · 34 99
ALDGATE EAST 36 00
ALDGATE 36
TOWER HILL 36 80
MINORIES Jn
LIVERPOOL STREET 40 81
MOORGATE 41 33
BARBICAN 41 96
FARRINGDON 40 18 · 44 32
KINGS CROSS ST. PANCRAS 44 17
EUSTON SQUARE 45 17
GREAT PORTLAND STREET 45 79
BAKER STREET 46 72
EDGWARE ROAD 47 44
PADDINGTON 48 26
BAYSWATER 49 24 · 49
ROYAL OAK 49 00
WESTBOURNE PARK 49 99
LADBROKE GROVE 50 79
LATIMER ROAD 51 44
NOTTING HILL GATE 50 03
GLOUCESTER ROAD 45 35
SOUTH KENSINGTON 44 63
SLOANE SQUARE 43 39
VICTORIA 42 35
ST. JAMES'S PARK 41 63
WESTMINSTER 40 87
EMBANKMENT 40 18
TEMPLE 39 48
BLACKFRIARS 38 72
MANSION HOUSE 38 12
CANNON ST. 37 81
MONUMENT 37 47

Line names:
DISTRICT LINE
PICCADILLY LINE
CIRCLE LINE
WEST LONDON LINE
WEST LONDON EXTENSION LINE
METROPOLITAN LINE
CIRCLE & DISTRICT LINES
DISTRICT AND PICCADILLY LINES
INNER RAIL / OUTER RAIL

Notes:
Earls Court Control Centre controls all the Piccadilly Line, also the District Lines from Ealing Broadway & Putney Bdge (WV, WY-E3, WD-PM)
Controlled by Baker St: Met & Jub Signalling Control Centre (MB-OJ-OB)
NR lines Moorgate—Kings+Thameslink controlled by West Hampstead (WH)
Controlled by NR from Wimbledon (W)
Midland City Line to Kentish Town
Apart from the Railway Engineering Workshop, most is out of use
* Change of Kilometrage
X = Experimental Shop
* at these km posts are actually on the other side
Full details of this area on 21A

Earls Court District
1 = EB LOCAL
2 = EB MAIN
3 = WB MAIN
4 = WB LOCAL

West Ken–Sth Ken.: the Piccadilly Line runs below the District Line

§ former Aldgate East + distance back from Rayners Lane
Aldgate East – Liverpool St 0.93km
Aldgate – Tower Hill 0.50km
45C: to Shoreditch
45C: to New Cross and New Cross Gate East London Line
km transfer point: District to London
36·2 Dist Line km
High St.Ken–Glouc Rd. 0.9km

MACHINE SHOP · Tool Room
SMITH SHOP · TRUCK SHOP · WHEEL SHOP
STORES
CARBODY SHOP B · PAINT SHOP · CARBODY SHOP A
HEAVY REPAIR SHOP
WOOD MILL · STORES
PLANT SHOP · MOTOR SHOP · ELECTRONICS
No.1 TRAVERSER · No.2 TRAVERSER
Test Track

continued on 43B
1A: to Willesden Junction
1A: to Clapham Junction
1A: to Kew Jns
1A: to Richmond
1A: to Waterloo
43: to Finchley Rd
43B: to Acton Town
3A: to Blackfriars
NR over to Paddington

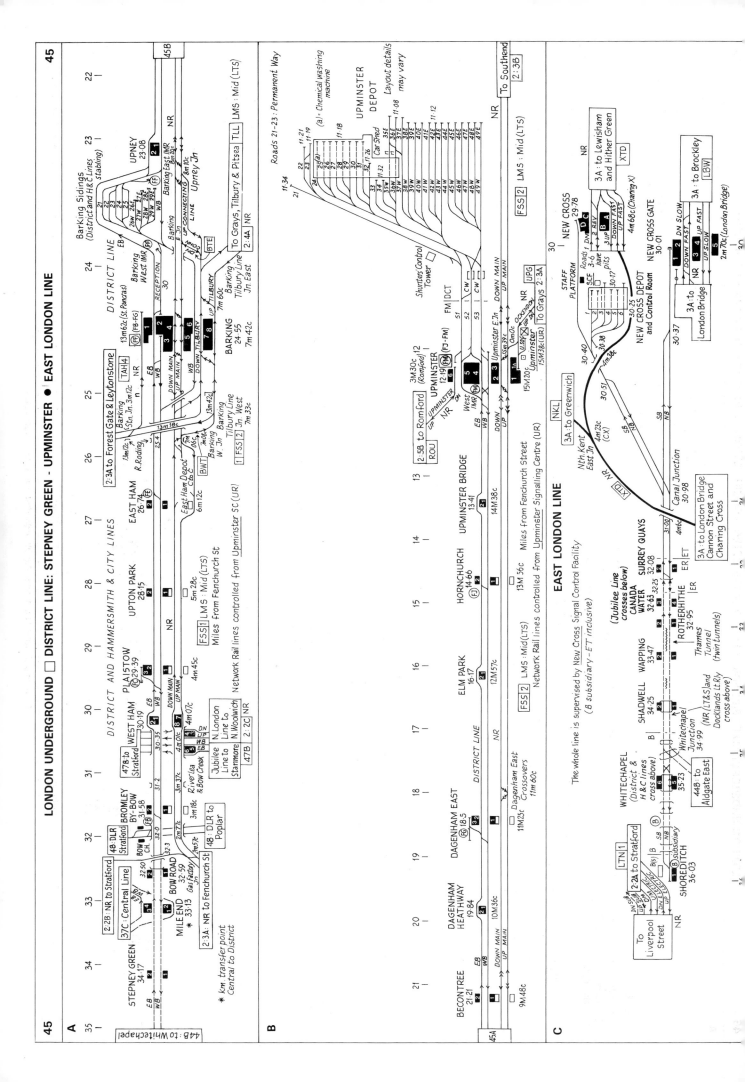

LONDON UNDERGROUND □ DISTRICT LINE □ DISTRICT LINE: STEPNEY GREEN - UPMINSTER ● EAST LONDON LINE

LONDON UNDERGROUND □ **PICCADILLY LINE: BARONS COURT - COCKFOSTERS** ● **POST OFFICE RAILWAY (MAIL RAIL)**

A

ø Holborn, Kings Cross, Finsbury Park – although line directions are Eastbound and Westbound, passenger information refers to 'Northbound' and 'Southbound' respectively

PB–PM controlled by Earl's Court Control Centre

46B

VICTORIA LINE
NB SB 33·18
EB WB 12

MANOR HOUSE 33·30

4OC: to Walthamstow

km. transfer point Piccadilly to Victoria

(ex GILLESPIE ROAD) 34·55 (VK)
ARSENAL 35·04 12

FINSBURY PARK ø 34·34

km. transfer point Piccadilly to Victoria

4OC: to Brixton

CALEDONIAN ROAD 36·38 21

HOLLOWAY ROAD 35·78 12

From Kings Cross to Finsbury Park the Piccadilly Line lies below the East Coast Main Line

km. transfer point Piccadilly to Northern

Kings Cross IMR

Northern Line 39B: to Euston

KINGS LOOP

RUSSELL SQUARE 39·26 1

YORK ROAD 37·7 Twin tubes

KINGS CROSS ST. PANCRAS ø 38·34 56
(Circle/H. & C/Met. and Victoria Lines cross above, the Northern Line below)

GREEN PARK 41·91
(Jubilee Line crosses below and Victoria Line above)

LEICESTER SQUARE 40·84
(Northern Line, CX crosses above)

HOLBORN ø 40·01
(Central Line crosses above)

COVENT GARDEN 40·58

ALDWYCH (closed 1 Oct. 1994) 40·84

PICCADILLY CIRCUS 41·37
(Bakerloo Line crosses above)

HYDE PARK CORNER 42·97

DOWN STREET 42·48

KNIGHTSBRIDGE 43·49

BROMPTON ROAD 44·2

SOUTH KENSINGTON 44·72
(Platform 4 above 3)

GLOUCESTER ROAD 45·42

EARLS COURT 46·22

EB PICCADILLY 47·41
WB PICCADILLY

EB DISTRICT
WB DISTRICT

BARONS COURT 47·84

From Barons Court tunnel mouth to South Kensington the Piccadilly Line lies below the District Line

44A: to Hammersmith

Twin tubes

TURNPIKE LANE 30·98

WOOD GREEN 29·99

BOUNDS GREEN 28·46

B

COCKFOSTERS DEPOT

PB – PM controlled by Earl's Court Control Centre

RECEPTION ROAD

CW Shed

East Cabn 29A

Cleaning Shed

Car Shed 54 53 52 51 50 49 48 47 46 45 44 43 42 41 40 39 38 37 36 35 34

West Cabn

COCKFOSTERS 22·04
22·42 22·39

EB WB Engrs 26 22·23

OAKWOOD 23·39 12

SOUTHGATE Viaduct 25·26 12
Southgate Tunnel (849m) 25·06

Twin tubes WB 24·9–24·7

Viaduct 25·91 EB 25·06

Viaduct 26·9 26·5

ARNOS GROVE 27·21

Arnos Grove Sidings 23
31 30 29 28 27 26 25

27·63 27·6 27·7 27·47 27·80 Viaduct

46A

C

MAIL RAIL

Owned by the Post Office

PB – PM controlled by Earl's Court Control Centre

former WESTERN DISTRICT OFFICE
(Western District Parcel Office)

WESTERN DISTRICT OFFICE (Rathbone Place)

WEST CENTRAL DISTRICT OFFICE

MOUNT PLEASANT

Control Rm

Mount Pleasant Depot
(150v DC overhead)

KING EDWARD BUILDING

LIVERPOOL STREET

EASTERN DISTRICT OFFICE

PADDINGTON 1859·9

349·3 909·9 740·6 1400·9 1367·1 1293 1731·9

L = Loco siding

2ft (·609m) gauge, 3rd rail 440v DC (150v in stations)

All underground. Double-track tunnels, except station approaches & platforms. Total length 10·5 km (6·5 miles)

Distances in metres between platform centres.

© Copyright Quail Map Company. No reproduction without permission

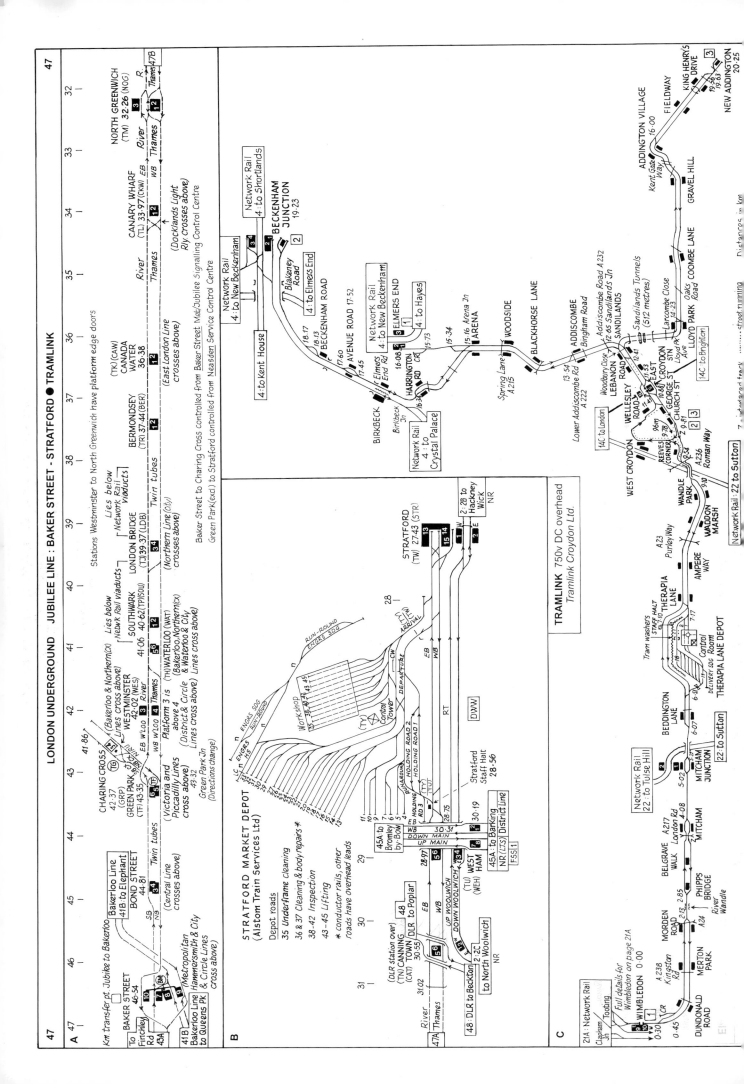

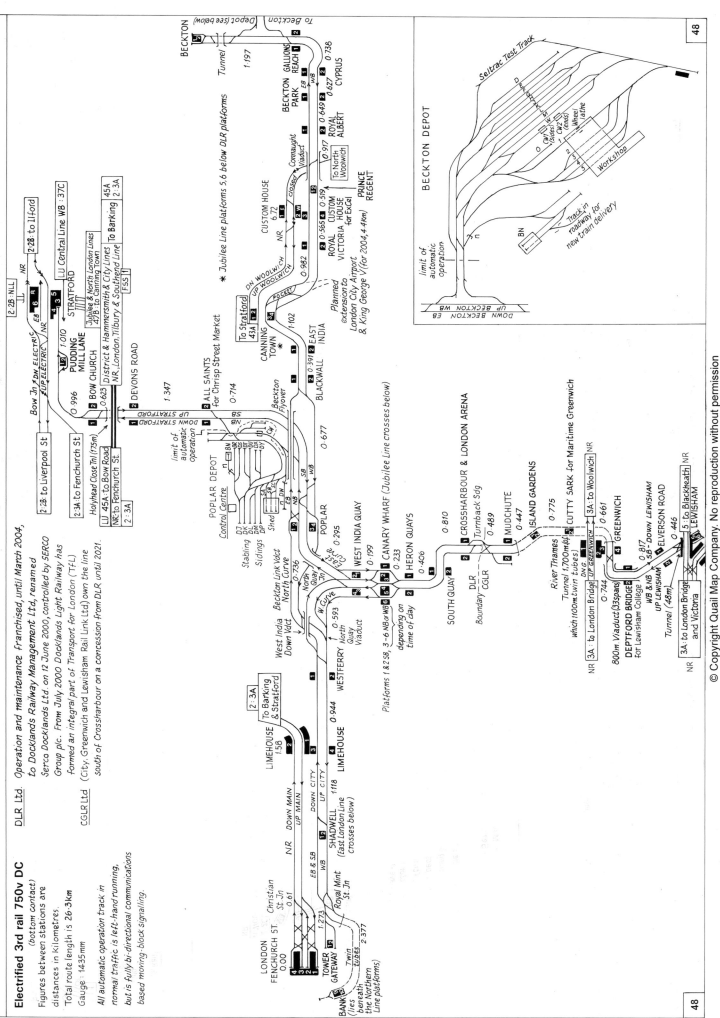

Electrified 3rd rail 750v DC
(bottom contact)

Figures between stations are distances in kilometres.

Total route length is 26·3km.

Gauge: 1435mm

All automatic operation track in normal traffic is left-hand running, but is fully bi-directional communications based moving-block signalling.

DLR Ltd. Operation and maintenance franchised, until March 2004, to Docklands Railway Management Ltd, renamed Serco Docklands Ltd. on 12 June 2000, controlled by SERCO Group plc. From July 2000 Docklands Light Railway has formed an integral part of Transport for London (TfL)

CGLR Ltd (City, Greenwich and Lewisham Rail Link Ltd) own the line south of Crossharbour on a concession from DLR until 2021.

BECKTON DEPOT

limit of automatic operation

Seltrac Test Track

Workshop

Wheel lathe

Track in roadway for new train delivery

DOWN BECKTON EB
UP BECKTON WB

48

© Copyright Quail Map Company. No reproduction without permission

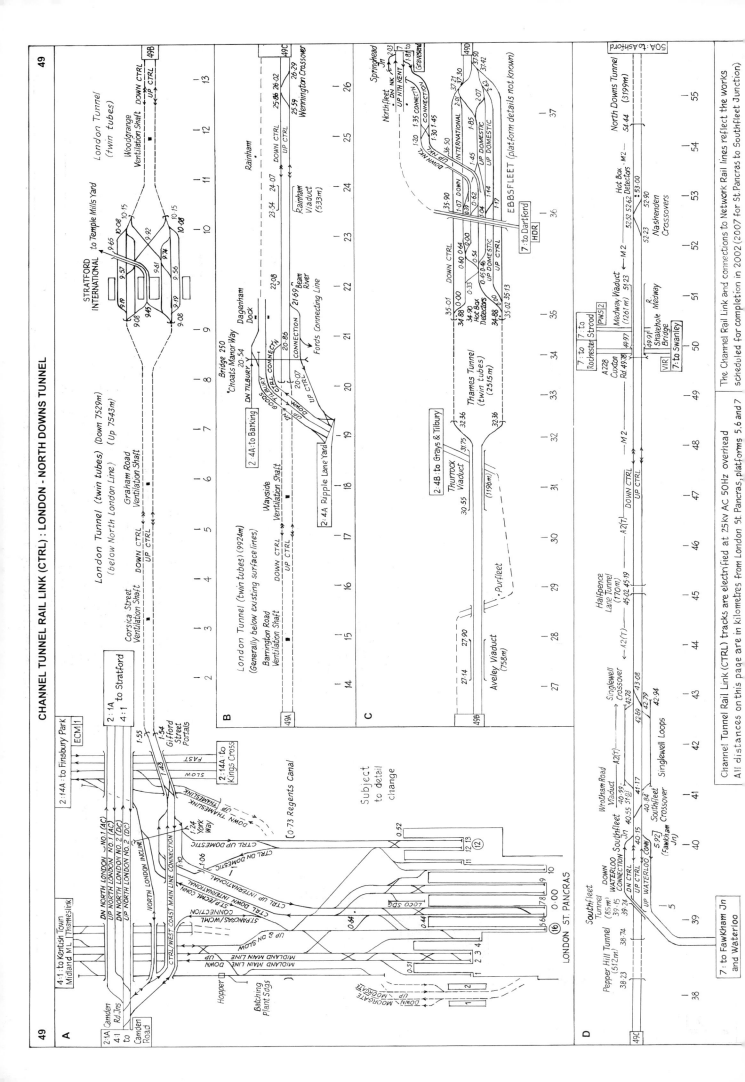

CHANNEL TUNNEL RAIL LINK (CTRL): LONDON - NORTH DOWNS TUNNEL

The Channel Rail Link and connections to Network Rail lines reflect the works scheduled for completion in 2002 (2007 for St. Pancras to Southfleet Junction)

Channel Tunnel Rail Link (CTRL) tracks are electrified at 25kv AC 50Hz overhead
All distances on this page are in kilometres from London St. Pancras, platforms 5, 6 and 7

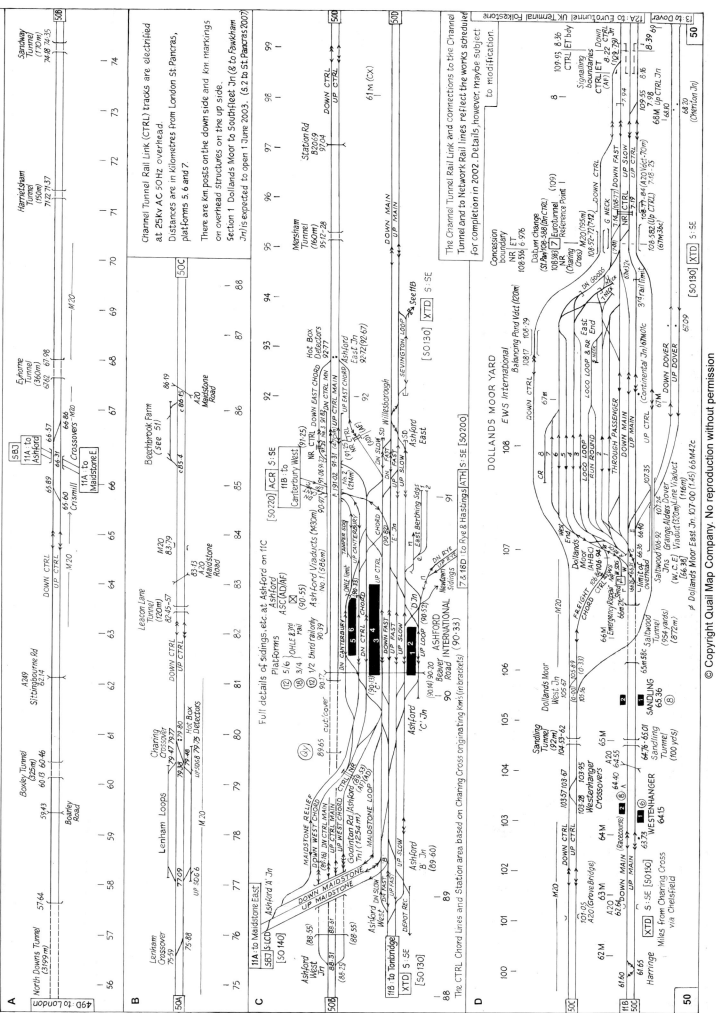

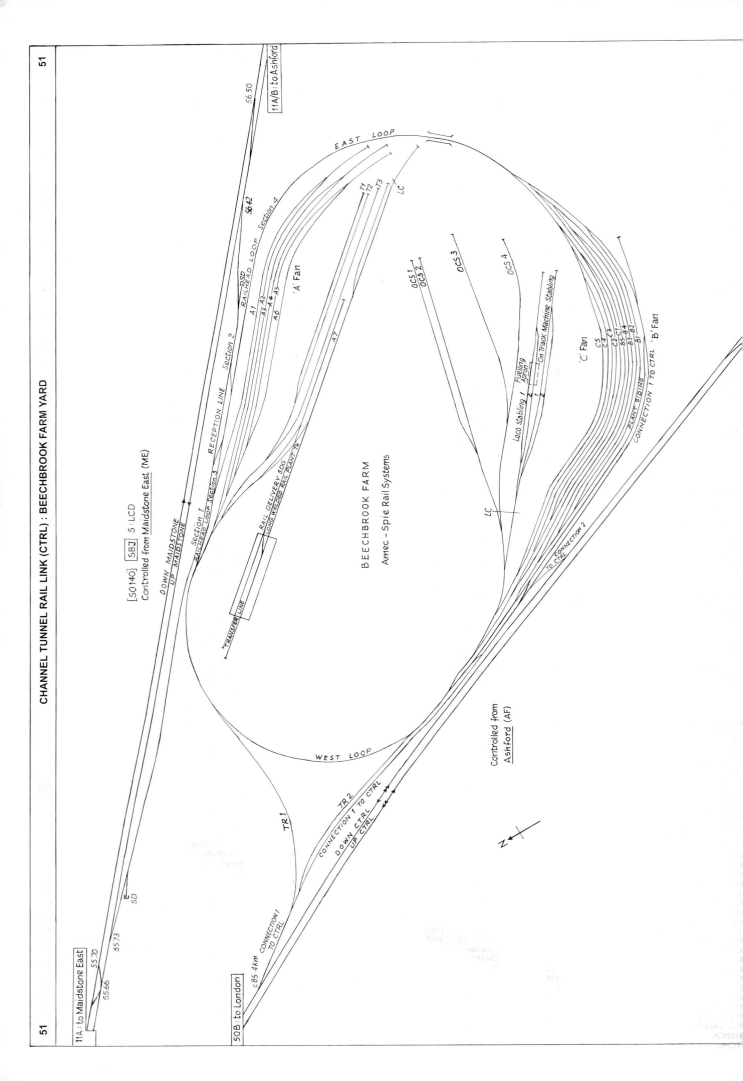

CHANNEL TUNNEL RAIL LINK (CTRL) : BEECHBROOK FARM YARD

IVERPOOL STREET	37C, 44B, 46C	NEWBURY PARK	38A	PUTNEY BRIDGE	44A
LOYD PARK	47C	NEWHAVEN HARBOUR	17A		
ONDON BLACKFRIARS	3A	NEWHAVEN MARINE	17A	QUEENSBOROUGH	8B
ONDON BRIDGE	3A, 39B, 47A	NEWHAVEN TOWN	17A	QUEENS PARK	41B
ONDON CANNON STREET	3A	NEWINGTON	8A	QUEEN'S ROAD, PECKHAM	3A
ONDON CHARING CROSS	3A	Nine Elms Junction	2	QUEENSBURY	42A
ONDON FENCHURCH STREET	48	NORBITON	21B	QUEENSTOWN RD (Battersea)	2
ONDON KENSINGTON OLYMPIA	1A, 44A	NORBURY	4	QUEENSWAY	37B
ONDON ROAD (Brighton)	16	NORDEN	35E	Quidhampton	32B
ONDON ROAD (Guildford)	23	NORMANS BAY	17B		
ondon Road Depot	41B	NORTH ACTON	37B	RAINHAM	8A
ONDON ST PANCRAS	49A	NORTH CAMP	24C	RAMSGATE	9A
ONDON VICTORIA	2	NORTH DULWICH	4	RAVENSBOURNE	4
ONDON WATERLOO	2	NORTH EALING	43B	RAVENSCOURT PARK	44A
ONGCROSS	25A	NORTH GREENWICH	47A	RAYNERS LANE	42A
ONGFIELD	7	NORTH HARROW	42A	RAYNES PARK	21A, 22
onghedge Junction	2	North Kent East Jn	3A	READING	27A
ards	43A	North Pole International Depot	1A	READING WEST	27A
OUGHBOROUGH JUNCTION	3A, 4	NORTH SHEEN	1A	Red Cow	34C
OUGHTON	38A	North Weald	38B	REDBRIDGE (Southampton)	30A
overs Walk	16	North Wembley	41A	REDBRIDGE (LU)	38A
OWER SYDENHAM	4	Northam Traincare Centre	29	REDHILL	15A
udgershall	32A	*NORTHERN LINE*	39, 40	REEDHAM	14C
ullingstone	6A, 7	NORTHFIELDS	43B	REEVES CORNER	14C, 47C
dd Town	18D	NORTHFLEET	7	REGENT'S PARK	41B
MINGTON PIER	30B	NORTHIAM	13A	REIGATE	15A
MINGTON TOWN	30B	NORTHOLT	37A	RICHMOND	1A
MPSTONE COMMANDO	34B	Northumberland Park Depot	40C	RICKMANSWORTH	41C
MPSTONE VILLIAGE	34B	NORTHWICK PARK	42A	RIDDLESDOWN	14C
		NORTHWOOD	42A	Ridham Dock	8B
AIDA VALE	41B	NORTHWOOD HILLS	42A	Riverside Yard	34C
AIDEN NEWTON	35A	NORWOOD JUNCTION	4, 14C	ROBERTSBRIDGE	18B
AIDSTONE BARRACKS	7	NOTTING HILL GATE	37B, 44B	ROCHESTER	7
AIDSTONE EAST	7	NUNHEAD	3A, 4	RODING VALLEY	38A
AIDSTONE WEST	7	NUTBOURNE	20D	ROLVENDEN	13A
AILRAIL	46C	NUTFIELD	10A, 15A	*ROMNEY, HYTHE & DYMCHURCH RLY*	18E
ALDEN &DISTRICT MODEL ENGINEERS	5A			ROMNEY SANDS	18E
ALDEN MANOR	22	OAKLANDS	36B	ROMSEY	32C
ANNEZ QUARRY	17C	OAKWOOD	46B	ROPLEY	24D
ANOR HOUSE	46A	OCKLEY	19A	*ROTHER VALLEY RAILWAY*	18B
ANSION HOUSE	44B	OLD KILN HALT	36B	ROTHERHITHE	45C
antles Wood	41C	*OLD KILN RAILWAY*	36B	ROWLANDS CASTLE	26B
ARBLE ARCH	37C	OLD STREET	39B	ROYAL ALBERT	48
archwood	30A	Ongar	38B	Royal Mint Street Jn	48
ARDEN	10C	ORE	18C	ROYAL OAK	44B
ARGATE	9A	ORPINGTON	6A	ROYAL VICTORIA	48
ARINA (BLACK ROCK)	16	OSTERLEY	43C	*ROYAL VICTORIA RLY*	29B
aritime Freightliner Terminal	30A	Osterley & Spring Grove	43C	RUISLIP	42A
arlborough Road	43A	OTFORD	6A, 7	Ruislip Depot	37A
ARTIN MILL	13	OVAL	40A	RUISLIP GARDENS	37A
ARTIN'S HERON	25B	OVERTON	27B	RUISLIP MANOR	42A
ARYLEBONE	41B	OXFORD CIRCUS	37C, 40B, 41B	RUSSELL SQUARE	46A
AZE HILL	3A	OXSHOTT	22	RYDE ESPLANADE	35C
EDSTEAD & FOUR MARKS	24D	OXTED	14B	RYDE PIER HEAD	35C
EOPHAM	7			RYDE ST. JOHNS RD	35C
ERSTHAM	15A	PADDINGTON	41B, 44B	RYE	18D
ERTON PARK	22,47C	PADDINGTON	46C	RYTHE HIGH LEVEL	5A
etropolitan Jns	3A	PADDOCK WOOD	10C		
ETROPOLITAN LINE	41C, 42.43A, 44B	*PALLOT HERITAGE STEAM MUSUEM*	36A	ST.DENYS	29
CHELDEVER	27C	PARK LANE	36D	ST. HELIER	22
D-HANTS RAILWAY	24D	PARK ROYAL	43B	ST. JAMES PARK	34C
LE END	37C, 45A	Parks Bridge Junction	34A	ST. JAMES'S PARK	44B
LFORD	26A	PARKSTONE	31A, 31B	ST. JOHNS	3A, 4
LL HILL EAST	39A	PARSONS GREEN	44A	ST. JOHNS WOOD	43A
LLBROOK	29	PASTON PLACE	16	ST. LEONARDS WARRIOR SQUARE	18C
LTON REGIS HALT	8C	PECKHAM RYE	3A, 4	St. Leonards West Marina	17B
nories Junction	44B	PENGE EAST	4	ST. MARGARETS	1A
INSTER	9A	PENGE WEST	4	ST. MARY CRAY	6A
TCHAM	22,47C	PENSHURST	10B	St. Mary's	44B
TCHAM JUNCTION	22,47C	PERIVALE	37B	ST. PAUL'S	37C
onkton & Came	31D	Perry Street Fork Jn	5	SALFORDS	15A
ontpelier Junction	16	PETERSFIELD	26B	SALISBURY	32B
ONUMENT	44B	PETTS WOOD	6A	Saltwood Jns	11C, 50D
OORGATE	39B, 44B	PEVENSEY BAY	17B	SANDERSTEAD	14C
OOR PARK	42A	PEVENSEY & WESTHAM	17A	SANDILANDS	47C
OORS VALLEY RAILWAY	33E	PHIPPS BRIDGE	22, 47C	SANDHURST	25B
ORDEN	40A	PICCADILLY CIRCUS	41B, 46A	SANDLING	11C, 50D
ORDEN ROAD	22, 47C	*PICCADILLY LINE*	43B, 43C, 44A, 46A, 46B	SANDOWN	35C
ORDEN SOUTH	22	Pig Hill Sidings	2	SANDWICH	9A
ORETON	31C	PIMLICO	40B	SANTA'S HALT	23A
ORNINGTON CRESCENT	39B	PINESWAY JUNCTION	36D	SEAFORD	17A
ORTIMER	27A	PINHOE	34B	SEATON	34D
ORTLAKE	1A	PINNER	42A	Seaton Junction	34A
OTSPUR PARK	22	Pirbright Jn	23	*SEATON TRAMWAY*	34D
OTTINGHAM	5	PLAISTOW	45A	SELHURST	4, 14C
OULSECOOMB	16	PLUCKLEY	10D	Selhurst Depot	14C
OUNT PLEASANT	46C	PLUMPTON	15C	SELLING	8B
untfield	18B	PLUMSTEAD	5	Selsdon	14C
UCH NATTER	36E	POKESDOWN	31A	Semley	33B
UDCHUTE	48	POLEGATE	17A	SEVEN SISTERS	40C
		POLSLOE BRIDGE	34B	SEVENOAKS	6A
shenden Crossovers	49D	POOLE	31B	Sevington Sidings	11B, 50C
ASDEN	42B	POPLAR	48	Shacklegate Junction	21B
asden Depot	42B	PORTCHESTER	26C	SHADWELL	45C, 48
asden Freight Terminal	1A	Portfield	20C	SHAKESPEARE STAFF HALT	13
TLEY	29	PORTSLADE	20A	SHALFORD	24A
W ADDINGTON	47C	PORTSMOUTH & SOUTHSEA	26C	SHANKLIN	35C
W BECKENHAM	4	PORTSMOUTH HARBOUR	26C	SHAWFORD	27C
w Copyhold Junction	15C	*POST OFFICE RAILWAY*	46C	SHEERNESS-ON-SEA	8B
W CROSS	3A, 45C	PRESTON PARK	16	SHEFFIELD PARK	35D
w Cross Depot	45C	PRESTON ROAD	42A	SHEPHERDS BUSH	37B, 44A
W CROSS GATE	3A, 45C	PRINCE REGENT	48	Shepherds Lane Junction	2, 3A, 4
W ELTHAM	5	PRINCESS ROYAL DISTRIBUTION CENTRE	1A	SHEPHERDS WELL	13
W HYTHE	7	PUDDING MILL LANE	48	SHEPPERTON	21B
W MALDEN	21A, 21B, 22	PULBOROUGH	19C	SHERBORNE	33C
W MILTON	31A	PURLEY	14C	SHOLING	29
W ROMNEY	18E	PURLEY OAKS	14C	SHOREDITCH	45C
w Wandsworth	4	PUTNEY	1A	SHOREHAM (Kent)	6A, 7

In the same series:
1 Scotland (2001) £7.50
2 England East (in preparation)
3 Western Region (2000) £7.50
4 Midlands & North West (in preparation) £8.95
The Quail Map Company produces and imports railway maps of various countries and cities. A catalogue will be sent on request.